# *Fishing In Oregon's*
# CASCADE LAKES

# *Fishing in Oregon's*
# CASCADE LAKES

## Scott Richmond

Flying Pencil Publications
Scappoose, Oregon

Published by Flying Pencil Publications in collaboration with Four
Rivers Press. Address all inquiries to:
Flying Pencil Publications
33126 Callahan Road
Scappoose, Oregon 97056
503-543-7171

Photographs by Scott Richmond unless credited otherwise. Maps by
Madelynne Diness Sheehan. Line drawings by Lora Crestwick. Cover art
by Guy Jacobson. Book and cover design by John Laursen.

Printed in the United States of America

10 9 8 7 6 5 4 3 2 1

Library of Congress Catalog Card Number: 94-070896

ISBN: 0-916473-09-0

*Limited edition prints of Guy Jacobson's cover art can be purchased
through Trails End Gallery, 16175 S.E. Highway 224, Clackamas, OR
97015; the phone is 503/658-2067.*

*To Barbara, the patient one*

## Acknowledgments

Lora Crestwick for the line drawings, some of which appeared previously in *The Pocket Gillie*. Madelynne Diness Sheehan for maps and editing. John Laursen for book and cover design. Guy Jacobson for cover art. Jim Dexter for review. Jed Davis for review of fishing with lures. Max Peel for review. Roger Neufeldt of Luhr Jensen for advice. Joann Frazee, John Hofferd, Mike Jewett, Norman and Roberta LaFleur, Don Knepper, Doug MacMillan, Pat Schatz, Bill Simmonds, and Larry Souza for advice. My wife Barbara for keeping the house and family running while I was gone.

The following people and agencies provided helpful information and review of certain portions of the manuscript: Ted Fies, John Fortune, Randy Henry, and Bob Hooten of the Oregon Department of Fish and Wildlife. Vicki Ramming and Jerry Vroman of the U. S. Forest Service.

## Publishers' Notice

Water-related sports and mountain travel are, by their very nature, hazardous. Risks include, but are not limited to, those related to terrain, weather, equipment, wild animals, errors in judgement, and physical limitations (not the least of which is the inability of humans to breathe while underwater). This book does not describe every hazard associated with fishing the Cascade Lakes and adjacent waters. Furthermore, despite our diligent efforts it may contain errors of typography, cartography, or content. This book's maps are for planning reference only, not for navigation. Flying Pencil Publications, Four Rivers Press, and the author shall have no liability or responsibility with respect to physical harm, property damage, or any other loss or damage asserted to be caused directly or indirectly by the information in this book. We sigh and regret that our society has reached such a litigious state that it is necessary to include a paragraph like this in a book about goin' fishin'.

# Contents

# Maps

# First Casts

If my mother were not quick thinking and intrepid, my first experience with lakes might have killed me.

When I was about 12 months old, my family lived in the eastern Washington town of Moses Lake. I had progressed from crawling to walking four months earlier, and now I was an energetic toddler, traveling through the wide, fascinating world with great mobility and not a lick of good sense. One summer day we went for a picnic beside a "pothole," one of those small, deceptively deep desert lakes that dot the sagebrush plains of the Inland Empire.

When Mom turned her back to get something from the basket, I ran into the lake. How was I to know I couldn't walk on water until I tried it? Mom turned around and saw me floating face-down several feet from shore.

My mother doesn't swim, but I was still close enough that she could wade in and just reach my foot. I was retrieved, wet but breathing. The arid desert soon dried me, although my mother's panic evaporated more slowly.

I've often wondered what I saw as I bobbed in that lake, staring into the water with a toddler's wide-eyed curiosity. I have no conscious recollection of this first experience with lakes, but I must have spied a fish and liked the look of it, for I've been fascinated with lakes and fish ever since.

Later, we moved to the Seattle area. We lived in several different houses as I grew up, but they were all within a few blocks of Lake Washington. For my seventh birthday, I was given a steel telescoping rod and an orange life jacket. My parents let me dangle a worm from a neighbor's dock, and there I caught my first fish, a yellow perch.

I was the proudest boy in three counties, more firmly hooked than that perch. I fell instantly in love with fishing and tried to convince some friends that dunking worms was more fun than baseball. They were dubious but went fishing with me anyway. For the next several years we fished anywhere we could find a friendly dock. Perch, chub, squawfish, bullheads, and even an occasional rainbow trout—it didn't matter what we caught so long as it had fins and slime.

My fishing gear was typical kid stuff: the venerable steel rod, now well-dented and thoroughly rusty; a reel that sounded like a car with bad brakes; a cork bobber; a #8 Eagle Claw worm hook tied to kinked-up ten-pound mono with six granny knots, and a Hills Brothers coffee can filled with dirt and worms. Half the guides were gone from the rod. Probably the only reason the rest didn't fall off was because they were glued down with rust. I had no concept that my tackle was junk or that better equipment existed.

As I neared puberty, some family friends invited me to go on a fishing trip. Mom and Dad discussed the condition of my tackle and concluded it was not only inferior, but socially embarrassing! I was given a spinning reel, a fiberglass rod, and a couple of Colorado spinners. It was cheap gear, costing about $7, but at least the rod wouldn't rust.

I ranged wider, caught more fish, read books and *Field and Stream*, got more sophisticated. Perch and chub were out, "real" game fish were

Lava Lake.

in. I bought a rod blank and built a tool worthy of trout and bass, saved my paper route profits and bought a Mitchell 304 spinning reel. I fished all year in Lake Washington, and summers I slipped on a backpack and trekked into the Cascades. As soon as the snow melted (and sometimes before), I tramped into any lake, tarn, or glacial cirque that had a trail, as well as a good many that didn't.

When I moved to Oregon and took up fly-fishing, it seemed natural that I would fish lakes with fly gear. I was surprised that most lake anglers viewed me as a quaint but harmless eccentric. Lakes were as comfortable to me as rivers, yet at that time most fly-anglers limited themselves to running water. Didn't they know how much fun lakes could be? Didn't they know how big fish can grow in a lake? Fortunately, more fly-fishers are now discovering the joys of casting their flies in lakes.

My favorite lakes are the desert waters of eastern Oregon and Washington, and Oregon's Cascade Lakes. I use the term "Cascade Lakes" loosely, meaning by it the lakes that lie on or near the Cascade Lakes Highway (also known as Century Drive) near Bend, plus the other popular nearby lakes: East, Paulina, Crescent, and Odell.

Not only do these eighteen lakes offer nine species of cold water game fish in abundance, but the quality of the fishing is superb, with trophy-sized fish available from several waters. To this, add spectacular mountain scenery, gorgeous forests, sunny weather, a wealth of well-kept campgrounds, and enough lodging, dining, and supply options to make an adventure comfortable. All this treasure is within a few hours of major metropolitan areas. Truly, this is an angler's heaven.

I think about these lakes all winter, planning the next season's trips. The hardest decision is choosing where to go first. "Lunker browns in Paulina?" I think. "Maybe some early season kokanee from Odell? But then there are those brook trout in Sparks. And the Atlantic salmon in Hosmer. And when Crane Prairie warms up, there are those giant rainbow; can't pass them up. But then Lava is a lot of fun, too. Then there's Cultus—I really enjoy fishing for mackinaw there. Maybe Davis is coming back and I should give it try . . ." And those are just a few of the early season options.

Then I start thinking about June damselflies, spoon and spinner fishing in July, riding my horse into the high lakes in August, those oh-so fussy midge hatches of September, and October's end-of-season feeding frenzy. After a few visits to the Cascade Lakes, you realize the biggest problem with fishing here: deciding which outstanding fishing opportunity to take advantage of.

When I go to these lakes, I have feelings of anticipation and excitement that are warm echoes from times past. They are the same feelings I had as a young boy heading out with a can of fresh-dug worms. Now I'm an adult, and my approach is more sophisticated. I usually carry at least two fly rods of considerable quality, enough reels to start a tackle store, four or five large boxes of flies, a spinning rod or two, a tackle box with hand-built spinners, spoons, and plugs, and more camera gear than I want my wife to know I own.

Out on a lake, I'll spend a lot of time peering into the water, trying to puzzle out what is going on in that liquid world. Sometimes, when I put aside the adult baggage of fancy tackle and analytic thinking, I see my reflection staring back, and it looks a bit like a care-free ten-year-old with a rusty steel rod. And sometimes I just close my eyes, and reaching deep into my self I try to imagine what it was like to be a toddler who found himself floating face down in a desert lake, getting his first wide-eyed glimpse of all the wonderful things that are in the water, captivated forever by all that he saw.

**My Approach to Fishing the Cascade Lakes.** Fishing is often magical, but there is no magic to fishing.

Every month or so I hear an exultant angler say something like, "I finally figured out the secret of catching Atlantic salmon in Hosmer Lake. You take a small fly on a long leader, and . . ." or, "I'll tell you what gets those giant browns in Paulina. Troll your plug at exactly . . ." I'm always interested in a fellow angler's success, and it's hard to ignore someone who talks like they just found the Lost Dutchman Mine. So I listen. These people often have some wisdom worth hearing, some nugget that will shed light on an aspect of fish behavior or angling technique.

But do they have THE secret of catching Atlantics in Hosmer Lake or brown trout in Paulina? No.

They don't have THE secret because there isn't one. There is no secret lure that is going to catch fish on every cast, no hidden holes filled with big trout, no mystical bait formula that will guarantee a rod-thumping lunker.

Our technology-based market-oriented culture promotes the belief that if you know some fact, or buy some object, all your problems will be solved. A lot of tackle is sold to people who believe they can buy

their way to fishing success.

But the key to successful fishing is not in "secrets," nor is it in anything you can buy. It is in what you understand about the fish and about their world. It's not what goes on the end of your leader that catches fish; it's what goes on between your ears.

Angling tactics should always be a response to what the water is telling us. When I approach a lake, whether it's an old friend or a new acquaintance, I try to slow down, put aside my prejudices, and absorb what the lake is telling me on this day, at this moment. Then I strive to stay alert to changing conditions such as wind direction, cloud cover, insect hatches, and water temperature.

Lakes are real talkers. They spin a never ending, always changing yarn about themselves. But because they are still waters, they speak with quiet voices. It takes a patient ear to hear their stories. In the end, what an angler needs most to be successful on lakes is patience, flexibility, a willingness to discard preconceived notions, and constant observation.

**How to Use This Book.** Lakes change. Some things are fairly constant, like the shape of the bottom, but other environmental factors change often. For instance, the Oregon Department of Fish and Wildlife (ODFW) may be stocking the lake with a different strain of rainbow trout, or the balance in the aquatic food chain may have shifted due to changes in water level, or some inlet creek may be dumping more cold water than usual into the lake because it was a wet winter, and so on.

Every lake in this book has altered significantly in the last decade, and will continue to change throughout the next. How should you respond to these changes? I feel that if you understand the environmental factors that affect fish, you can recognize changing conditions and adapt your tactics to them. That way you will always be more successful than those unimaginative anglers who blindly fish in the same places with the same tactics hour after hour, in every season, year after year.

Therefore, in this guidebook I explain *why* you should fish somewhere and *why* some approaches work better than others.

Eighteen lakes are described in Chapter 2. These are the most popular lakes in the area, and all of them can be reached (or nearly reached) by car. Fourteen of them are on or near the Cascade Lakes Highway (road 46).

Fishing the high lakes—those lakes in the Deschutes National Forest that are reached by walking or by remote roads—is discussed briefly in Chapter 3. Chapter 4 is a bonus section that describes fishing Fall River and the upper Deschutes River, which are in the same vicinity as the Cascade Lakes.

Chapters 5-7 cover lake fishing techniques appropriate to the Cascade Lakes. Chapter 5 presents subjects of general interest, like how to find fish. Chapter 6 discusses fly-fishing tactics for these lakes.

Chapter 7 describes how to fish the lakes with bait and lures. I admit quite freely that I am more at home with a fly rod than with other tackle, and 75% of my fishing in these lakes is done with flies. So for this chapter I have enlisted the assistance of those who are experts with bait and lure.

**Other Resources.** Here are some other valuable books for anglers bound for the Cascade Lakes:

*Strategies for Stillwaters,* by Dave Hughes, is an outstanding resource for any fly-fisher who wants to be successful in lakes. This is a superb

book, both useful and entertaining.

*Lake Fishing with a Fly,* by Ron Cordes and Randall Kaufmann, is another great book for fly-anglers.

*Spinner Fishing for Steelhead, Salmon, and Trout,* by Jed Davis, is the best reference on fishing with spinners. Jed's thorough and unique approach is useful to all anglers.

*Western Hatches*, by Rick Hafele and Dave Hughes, and *Aquatic Insects and Their Imitations*, by Rick Hafele and Scott Roderer, are both excellent sources of information about the aquatic insects that live in western waters.

*Flies: The Best One Thousand*, by Randle Stetzer, and *The Fly Tiers Nymph Manual* and *Tying Dry Flies* by Randall Kaufmann, are my favorite references for fly patterns.

*Fishing in Oregon*, by Madelynne Diness Sheehan and Dan Casali, is a complete guide to all fishing water in the state. It gives a good overview of other rivers and lakes that you might want to visit while in the area.

*The Pocket Gillie*, by Scott Richmond, is a vest-pocket handbook for fly-fishers of all abilities. It gives details on aspects of fly-fishing that are only briefly touched on in this book. Take it with you when you fish the rivers and lakes of North America, and use it to help you locate receptive trout, choose the right fly, and present it with confidence.

**Services.** Services available to anglers are summarized below. This is not an exhaustive list, by any means, and keep in mind that some of these businesses will no doubt change over the next few years. All phone numbers are within area code 503.

*Tackle Dealers and Fly Shops.* In addition to the retailers listed here, many general purpose stores in the area have a small tackle section, and all the resorts have some tackle (see Chapter 2)

Bi-Mart. 351 NE 2d, Bend. 389-5505.

Deschutes Fly and Tackle. 15746 Burgess Rd, La Pine. 536-1441.

Deschutes River Outfitters (fly shop). 61115 S. Highway 97, Bend. 388-8191.

Dexter's Fly Shop. 52582 Highway 97, La Pine. 536-9038.

Fred Meyer. 61535 S. Highway 97, Bend. 385-6648.

GI Joe's. 63455 N. Highway 97, Bend. 388-3778.

Hook Wine and Cheddar. Sunriver Village Building 22. 593-1633.

Payless Drug Store. 2050 NE 3d (Highway 97), Bend. 389-1113, and 700 SE 3d (highway 97), Bend. 389-9718.

The Fly Box. 923 SE 3d (Highway 97), Bend. 388-3330.

The Patient Angler (fly shop). 2524 NE Division, Bend. 389-6208.

*U. S. Forest Service.* The Forest Service is responsible for most of the roads and campgrounds in the Cascade Lakes area. They are a good source of information, such as which roads are open (check early and late in the season). Maps and brochures are also available from the Forest Service. The Deschutes National Forest, which contains all the water discussed in this book, is divided into ranger districts. East and Paulina lakes are in the Fort Rock Ranger District (503-388-5674). Crescent and Odell lakes are in the Crescent Ranger District (503-433-2234). All other waters are in the Bend Ranger District (503-388-5664).

*Central Oregon Chamber of Commerce.* The Chamber provides visitors with free guide books on lodging and dining in the area. It also has brochures on other area activities, such as rafting, llama backpacking, dude ranches, bird watching, and points of interest.

The Chamber can be reached at 503-382-3221, or write or visit their office at 63085 N. Highway 97, Bend, OR 97701.

*Oregon Guides and Packers.* Oregon Guides and Packers is a state-wide organization of professional guides and outfitters. Call them at 503-683-9552, or write to PO Box 10841, Eugene, OR 97440. They will send you a free 80-page booklet listing fishing and hunting guides, white water outfitters, horse packers, and other outdoor professionals in Oregon.

*Maps.* The Forest Service has a large map covering the Deschutes National Forest. It shows many of the roads for the area. The U. S. Geological Survey has topographic maps that are a much larger scale and have contour lines. Be aware that the topographic maps are updated infrequently, so they do not always show current roads accurately.

Forest Service maps are available from the Forest Service, or at many outdoor stores.

*Oregon Department of Fish and Wildlife.* Weekly fishing reports can be heard on the telephone by calling 1-800-275-3474 (1-800-ASK-FISH).

# 1
# Being There

The Cascade Lakes area is "user-friendly." Each of the eighteen lakes detailed in this book has at least one campground. Many (but not all) of the campgrounds have drinking water. Nine of the lakes also boast a resort, and some of the resorts have a restaurant to rescue those who have tired of camp cooking.

Recreationists should keep in mind they are in an alpine region a mile or so above sea level. Summer weather can be quite warm and pleasant, but it can also be cold, wet, and windy. I have spent July days huddled in my sleeping bag for warmth while I listened to rain pounding on the tent, and have sweated buckets in October. Come prepared for extremes in any season. Make sure you have suitable clothing for everyone in your party, and that your camping gear can stand both wind and rain.

There are few dangerous animals in the region, but mosquitoes can be a nuisance. Many campers have pitched their tent by a pretty lakeside meadow and later come to suspect that "meadow" is an old Indian word meaning "beautiful flat grassy place with billions of whining, blood-sucking pests." Some lakes have more mosquitoes than others, but you should always be prepared with lots of repellent.

**Getting There.** Most of the roads in the Cascade Lakes area are maintained by the U. S. Forest Service. They use a very logical system to identify roads, as follows. A primary road has a two digit number, such as "46." A secondary road is identified by a four digit number, where the first two digits tell you which primary road it intersects. For instance, road 4630 is a secondary road that intersects road 46.

Most primary roads are paved. Some secondary roads are paved, but many others are gravel. Primary and secondary roads are in good shape and suitable for most automobiles.

Spur roads are short segments. They are identified with seven digits, where the first four tell which road it intersects. For example, 4636-680

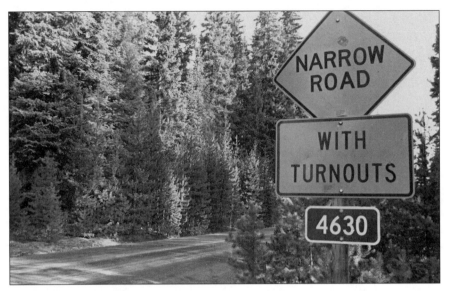

Secondary roads are identified with four digits, where the first two are the primary road it intersects. Here, secondary road 4630 begins at primary road 46.

Spur roads have seven digits, where the first four show the primary or secondary road they intersect.

is a spur road that intersects road 4636, and 4600-200 is a spur that intersects road 46. Spur roads are of variable quality. Some lead to large campgrounds and are paved. Some lead nowhere and are extremely rough single-lane dirt roads—real "coffee spillers," with washouts and maybe a tree or two across them. The "access" section for each lake describes the quality of spur roads that can be used to reach a lake.

Some areas have logging roads cut through them. These roads look like they were laid out by a drunken sailor. You can easily get lost and confused on them, and none lead to water anyway. So if you find yourself on a dirt road traveling through a logged-off area, back-track until you reach a numbered Forest Service road.

**Camping.** Over 70 public campgrounds and recreation sites are described in this book. All but one, La Pine State Recreation Area, are under the jurisdiction of the U. S. Forest Service. I mention only those that directly serve the lakes and rivers described. For a complete list of all campgrounds in the Deschutes National Forest, contact the Forest Service at 503-388-5664.

Most of these campgrounds have similar facilities: drinking water, pit toilets (outhouses), a dumpster for trash, and designated and numbered

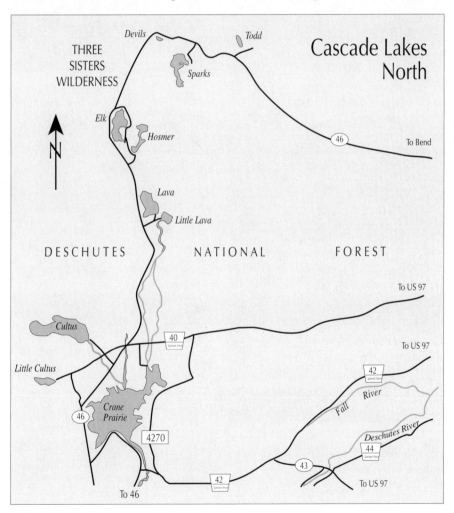

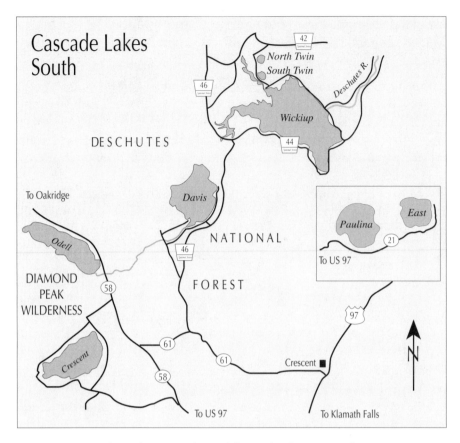

Cascade Lakes
South

North Twin
South Twin
Deschutes R.
42
46
Wickiup
44
DESCHUTES
To Oakridge
Davis
Paulina
East
Odell
NATIONAL
46
21
To US 97
DIAMOND
PEAK
WILDERNESS
58
FOREST
97
61
61
Crescent
Crescent
58
N
To US 97
To Klamath Falls

camp sites, each with a wooden table and a fire pit with a swing-away grate.

Some campgrounds have one or two boat ramps, and many of these have a small dock to facilitate loading and unloading boats. A day-use area is often located near a boat ramp. Day-use areas usually have wooden tables and barbecues.

Not all campgrounds have these facilities, however. Some are primitive and have a only a few tables and a pit toilet, and some have even less. When I describe a campground, you can assume that it has the "usual" facilities: drinking water, pit toilets, trash dumpster, designated sites with a table and a steel or concrete fire pit. Any amenities besides these are mentioned. If it is a primitive campground, I state the fact and list only those facilities that are present. Unless stated otherwise, there is a fee for each night you stay. At this time, fees range from $6 to $10 per night.

Camp sites in Forest Service campgrounds usually include a table and a fire pit.

In the past, many of the most popular campgrounds had a resident host for the summer. However, the Forest Service has arranged for a private firm to manage the campgrounds and collect fees. Thus, the hosts will probably be eliminated at all campgrounds except Mallard Marsh on Hosmer Lake.

Two of the campgrounds mentioned here have facilities for those who bring horses or other pack or riding stock. Reservations are required for these campgrounds. In addition, there are three group camps for which reservations must be made.

Other than the horse and group camps, you cannot make advance reservations for any campground. Sites are strictly first-come-first served, and during peak use periods on holidays and from mid-June through mid-July, they can fill up quickly beginning on Thursday night.

**Campground Rules.** The Forest Service has a few rules about staying in its campgrounds. These include:

*Do not clean fish, dishes, or do personal washing* near a

Most campgrounds have pit toilets (outhouses).

Fish cleaning stations are available at many campgrounds. They are good places to prepare your catch for the frying pan.

Animals are not welcome on swimming beaches, so leave Fido at camp or in the car.

drinking water faucet or pump.

*Do not build a fire* except in a fire pit or fire ring.

*Do not set off fireworks.*

*Keep dogs on a leash.*

*Do not bring a dog or other animal* onto swimming beach areas.

Besides the official Forest Service rules, there are some guidelines that should be followed in campgrounds and recreation sites:

*Drive especially slowly* (about 5 mph) in areas that are not paved; any faster and you raise dust that blows into camp sites.

*When driving through or near campgrounds,* watch for small children. While parents are distracted by other things, their excited children run around without looking where they're going. Give them a brake.

*Put food and garbage away in a solid container,* especially at night. Otherwise you will be visited by critters such as gray jays, chipmunks, squirrels, raccoons, and maybe even a black bear.

Message boards are placed at many road junctions and campground entrances so friends can find each other.

**Dealing with bear problems.** The Deschutes National Forest has black bears, especially in the Newberry Crater area near East and Paulina lakes. Bears are a natural part of the alpine environment. They do not want to eat anglers for dinner, but they can be a nuisance around campgrounds.

There are some obvious no-nos, like don't sleep with a slab of bacon in your tent. Here are some other guidelines for dealing with bears.

*Don't leave food or garbage around,* especially at night; this includes scraps around your fire ring. A bear has a nose about 10,000 times more sensitive than a human's (I'm not making this up) and can smell food even if it's in a cooler. Bears regard coolers as a kind of pistachio nut; they rip the lid off to get at the goodies inside. Put the food in your car or RV and you should have no problems.

*Keep your dog on a leash and locked up at night.* Dogs cannot resist barking at bears, and bears find dogs unusually aggravating.

*If you spot a bear,* don't move in close to take pictures. Keep your distance.

*Under no circumstances whatsoever should you feed a bear.*

**Resorts.** There are ten resorts at lakes covered in this book. They are at the following lakes: Crane Prairie, Crescent, Cultus, East, Elk, Lava, Odell (has two resorts), Paulina, and South Twin. These resorts are for the convenience of the public and are privately operated under Forest

Service leases. Their services vary and are described in the "Campgrounds and Services" section for the lake at which they are located.

If your idea of a "resort" is a modern architect-designed facility with golf courses, swimming pools, French chefs, designer boutiques, and every amenity desired by man, woman, or child, then you should stay at some place like Sunriver. The resorts at the lakes can be quite pleasant and comfortable, but they are simple, often rustic affairs meeting the basic needs of anglers and families.

## At a glance.

*Resorts with RV parks:* Crane Prairie, Lava, Twin Lakes/Wickiup, East, Shelter Cove (Odell).

*Lakes good for canoes, kayaks, and float tubes:* Todd, Devils, Sparks, Hosmer, South Twin, North Twin.

*Fly-fishing-only waters:* Davis, Hosmer, Sparks, Fall River.

*Lakes with trophy brown trout:* Paulina, East, Wickiup.

*Lakes with trophy rainbow trout:* Crane Prairie, Davis (eventually).

*Lakes with kokanee:* Paulina, Odell, Wickiup, East, Crescent, Elk, Crane Prairie.

*Lakes with mackinaw:* Odell, Crescent, Cultus.

*Lakes with Atlantic salmon:* Hosmer, East, Davis.

*Lakes with largemouth bass:* Crane Prairie.

# 2

# The Lakes

What words best describe these lakes? Certainly *abundance* and *quali-ty* apply. *Beauty* and *accessibility* come to mind. But my favorites are *uniqueness* and *variety*.

Some of the variety comes from the nine species of cold water game fish you can find here. Beyond this, however, there are varieties of size, scenery, isolation, popularity, access, campgrounds, resorts, and so forth.

Because of this variety, no two bodies of water are exactly alike. Each lake offers a unique angling experience. Even the two lakes that are most like each other, North and South Twin, are different. While their size is similar and they are only a quarter mile apart, South Twin has a fully developed campground and a resort, and North Twin is more rustic. There are even some differences in the way the two lakes should be fished.

Therefore, the best advice I can give to anyone bound for the Cascade Lakes is this: recognize that each lake you come to is unique, and your goal as an angler should be to pay close attention to what the lake has to say about itself so you can unlock its individuality. If you fish one lake exactly the same way you fish another, you are missing the op-portunities it offers you.

Eighteen lakes are described in detail in this chapter. Fourteen of them are just off, or not far from, the Cascade Lakes Highway (Forest Road 46, sometimes known as Century Drive). Odell and Crescent lakes, two waters that are near the end of this road, are included, as are East and Paulina lakes, which are in the general area. Except for Todd Lake, which requires a short walk, all these lakes can be reached by good roads.

Lakes are described in alphabetical order. For each lake, there is a brief description followed by sections on access to the lake, camp-grounds and recreation sites, and how to fish the lake. The *How To* section assumes familiarity with Chapters 5-7. When a campground is described, you can assume it has the standard Forest Service amenities (designated sites with table and fire pit, drinking water, pit toilets, trash dumpster, overnight fee) unless mentioned otherwise.

Fishing and boating regulations are summarized for each lake, but anglers should be aware that the rules may be changed without notice, and that this book is not the authority. Fishing regulations are updated every year, and you should always check the current Oregon angler's synopsis. Also, special regulations may be in effect, so read posted signs for new rules.

## Crane Prairie Reservoir

Size: 3,420 acres     Elevation: 4,445 feet

Seventy years ago, Crane Prairie really was a prairie, not a lake. The Deschutes River flowed through it and was joined by five other streams: Cultus River, Cultus Creek, Quinn River, Deer Creek, and Rock Creek. The Deschutes was first dammed here in 1922, but a new dam was built in 1940. The dam flooded six square miles of prairie so the water could be stored and used for summer irrigation.

The flat surface of the old Crane Prairie was a mix of meadow and forest. The trees were not logged before the flood gates closed, and many of the dead snags still stand, giving the lake an eerie, sculptural feel. Many snags have fallen and become part of the bottom structure of Crane Prairie. They provide cover for fish and habitat for abundant aquatic life such as damselflies, mayflies, and leeches. The shallow depth of the lake, combined with a rich inflow of nutrients, allows robust growth of aquatic vegetation.

This lush underwater habitat has made Crane Prairie Reservoir one of the most productive rainbow trout fisheries in Oregon. This is water where a five-pound trout generates yawns from locals. If you want their attention, you'd better hook one of the ten-pounders.

Not all the critters here are in the water, however. Crane Prairie is a wildlife management area, and it is estimated that half of all the osprey that live in Oregon have nests at Crane Prairie. The big raptors can be seen sitting in snags, or circling overhead looking for fish. When an osprey spots a fish near the surface, it hovers briefly, then plummets from 100 feet or more and hits the water with a smack and a splash. Usually the big bird will fly away with a trout or bass in its talons. It sure looks

Many tree trunks still stand in Crane Prairie and provide habitat for trout.

like a fun way to fish!

Bald eagles, great blue herons, and cormorants are also common sights at Crane Prairie. It offers a unique wealth of water-oriented life.

**Access.** Road 4270 passes near the east shore of Crane Prairie. Three spur roads lead off it and end at the lake, as described below. There are several other spur roads off road 4270, but they end at locked gates far from the water.

A short paved spur off 4270 goes to the resort and Crane Prairie Campground. There are signs for both on 4270.

Road 4270-475 is 0.4 miles south of the resort turn-off (there is no sign for this road). It is single-lane dirt and very rough, especially near the end where sharp lava rock can easily shred a tire or two. The road reaches the lake in 0.6 miles. If you can get there, it is a good spot to do a little bank fishing or to launch a canoe. It is also one of the best places for a fly-fisher to launch a float tube and kick over to the snags for some good fishing with damselfly nymphs. This road is not suited to trailered craft or large RVs.

Road 4270-200 is two miles south of the turn-off to the resort (no sign). It starts out as gravel and turns to rough single-lane dirt after a half mile. The road ends at the lake 1.1 miles from road 4270. There is access to the lake and a rough boat launch 0.6 miles from 4270.

Road 4285 is a four-mile long road that runs along the southern

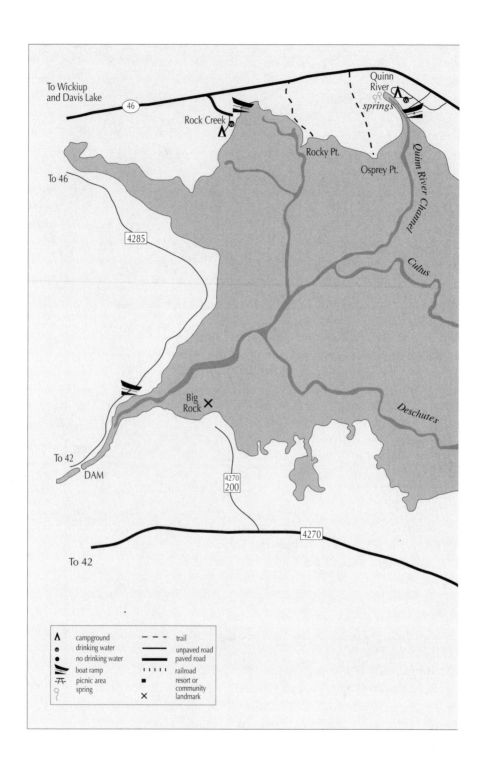

To Wickiup
and Davis Lake

46

Rock Creek

Quinn
River

*springs*

Rocky Pt.

To 46

Osprey Pt.

*Quinn River Channel*

4285

*Cultus*

Big
Rock ✕

*Deschutes*

To 42

DAM

4270
200

4270

To 42

| | | | |
|---|---|---|---|
| Λ | campground | - - - | trail |
| � | drinking water | ——— | unpaved road |
| ● | no drinking water | ▬▬▬ | paved road |
| ⚓ | boat ramp | ı ı ı ı ı | railroad |
| ⊼ | picnic area | ■ | resort or |
| ⚲ | spring | ✕ | community landmark |

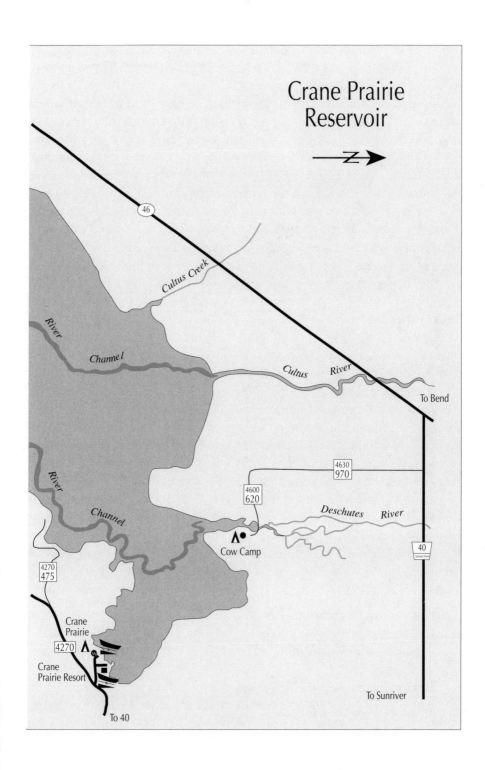

# Crane Prairie
# Reservoir

46

Cultus Creek

River

Channel

Cultus    River

To Bend

River

4630
970

4600
620

Channel

Deschutes    River

Λ•
Cow Camp

40

4270
475

Crane
Prairie

4270   Λ
       W.

Crane
Prairie Resort

To Sunriver

To 40

shore of the lake between roads 46 and 42. Near road 46, it is dirt and very rough, but most of the rest is gravel, although heavily washboarded. This road has numerous spurs to the lake. Many of these spurs are very rough dirt roads unsuitable for most vehicles. About three-quarters mile from 42, the road passes near the dam that creates the lake; camping and fishing are not permitted near the dam. There is an outhouse and a concrete boat ramp 1.1 miles from the junction with 42. Because this ramp is near the dam, it is in an area that always has sufficient water for launching, regardless of the water level in the rest of the reservoir.

Where road 42 crosses the Deschutes River, there is a fishing platform for the handicapped. Fishing closes here on September 1 each year, but it is a good area for viewing spawning kokanee from Wickiup Reservoir. Eagles can sometimes be seen feeding on dead kokanee.

Road 46 passes the southwest side of Crane Prairie. There are well-signed turn-offs here for the Rock Creek and Quinn River campgrounds, and Osprey Point.

About 100 feet south of the entry to Rock Creek Campground there is a rough single-lane dirt road that loops over to the lake. The Forest Service plans to close this road to public access.

There is a turn-out at a blocked road 0.6 miles north of the Rock Creek entry, on the west side of road 46. You can park here, but do not block the gate because the road is used by the Forest Service. From here, you can take a trail three-eighths mile east to a rocky point. This is a good place to fish (sometimes), and the trail is often used by float tubers seeking to avoid a long kick from the campground.

Road 40 (paved) intersects road 46 north of the lake. A bit east of this intersection, a short gravel spur—4000-970—proceeds south and joins road 4600-620. Turn left and you will soon enter Cow Meadow Campground on the Deschutes River just north of the lake. It is possible to take a canoe down the river into the lake, but other craft will not be able to make the trip.

**Campgrounds, Recreation Sites, and Services.** The section on access to Crane Prairie describes how to get to several primitive areas that can be used by self-sufficient campers. Established campgrounds and the resort are described here.

*Crane Prairie Resort.* This is sometimes called "Gales Landing," in reference to its past. The store has just about anything a Crane Prairie angler needs. The resort's phone number is 503-383-3939; the mailing address is PO Box 1171, Bend, OR 97709. Services include:

 RV park with 31 full-hookup spaces and 10 camp sites

 Store with sundries, limited groceries, and extensive bait and
   tackle, including flies

 Boat and motor rental

 Moorage

 Fishing guide service

 Showers and laundromat

 Gas and propane

 Emergency phone

*Crane Prairie Campground.* This is the mother of all campgrounds. There are 146 designated sites on paved roads so circuitous they provide maps so you won't get lost. Four camp sites are barrier free for the handicapped. Sites 91-96 are for tents only.

There are two large concrete boat ramps, each with a dock. One ramp is near the day-use area between the campground and the resort. It is a double-wide ramp, so two boats can be launched at once. There is a fish cleaning station here, and the trailer parking area is huge.

The second boat ramp is on the "blue" loop. It has room for only one boat at a time. A fish cleaning station is next to site 104.

A day-use area is located between the resort and the trailer parking area. It has tables and barbecues. Water and toilets are nearby.

*Rock Creek Campground.* There are 32 designated sites here. Sites 1-9 are near the lake along a dirt road; they are spread out for privacy and are good for tent campers. The remaining sites are on paved cul-de-sacs. While the cul-de-sacs are well separated, the sites within each cul-de-sac are close together, so this part of the campground is suited to groups who want to stay near each other. There is a message board at the campground entrance.

The paved boat ramp is provided with handicapped parking. Ample trailer parking for others is available near the fish cleaning station. When the water level is very low, the end of this ramp does not reach the lake, and it is very easy to get your vehicle stuck in the mud.

*Quinn River Campground.* Forty-one sites are spread over enough area to give some privacy. The usual Forest Service facilities are provided. There is a message board where the road splits for the camping and boat ramp areas.

The concrete boat ramp puts you in the Quinn River several hundred yards from the lake. Except in very low water, or for very deep

Crane Prairie Resort has everything you need for a good day of fishing. The resort also offers an RV park with full hookups.

boats, there is sufficient river water for access to the lake. However, you need to watch for occasional sunken logs in the river.

There is a large trailer parking area near the boat ramp. A pit toilet is near the parking area. The toilet is equipped for the handicapped, but a handicapped ramp is not provided.

*Cow Meadow.* This is a primitive campground with no fee. A few tables and fire pits are available, as are pit toilets. Trash pickup and drinking water are not provided.

**How to Fish Crane Prairie**. The primary fish species in Crane Prairie is rainbow trout. There are also a few brook trout and even some kokanee. The rainbow can reach six pounds in three or four years because the lake is so productive.

Largemouth bass were illegally introduced in the mid-1980s by that special breed of pond scum that can't stand to see a weedy body of water without their favorite fish. These people take matters into their own hands, the rest of the world be damned. I'm pretty bummed about the bass in Crane Prairie, which seem to be leaking through the dam and into Wickiup. I'm not going to talk about them other than to say that they are mostly in the south end where the water is warmer, some of them are pretty big, and that you should kill as many as you legally can.

Both trout and bass can be caught throughout the fishing season if you understand their needs and how they adapt to changing conditions. May is the best time of year for numbers of fish, but September is when the biggest fish are caught. The lake is most crowded from mid-June to mid-July.

This is a civilized body of water, where you can sleep late if you want. There is a short early morning bite, but after that, fishing usually slows down until 10 AM and can stay strong until around 5 PM. Evening activity can be good, but tends toward smaller fish.

Crane Prairie is a big body of water, and a first-time visitor may feel daunted by its size. It seems like the fish could be anywhere. Sometimes they are! Early in the season they scatter throughout the lake, and the best places to look for them are among the standing timber. As the lake warms, fish will concentrate in the north end because of the cool inflow from the Deschutes.

In the height of summer, the trout are found mostly in the old river channels. The map gives an idea of where the channels are located, but unless the water is clear they are hard to pinpoint without a depth finder. Often, the channels are only three to five feet deeper than the rest of the bottom, so you can't always identify them looking down from above.

As the water cools at the end of the season, the trout tend to scatter again.

Pat Schatz, owner of Crane Prairie Resort, has fished the lake for many years. He says that every year he finds fish in different places because of changing conditions. Pat feels that if you can't get any action after 30 minutes in one place, you should try a new spot.

This lake is productive, but like all lakes, it is subject to change. Therefore, anglers need to experiment and not just fish the same old favorite holes, figuring if they get no action the "fish just aren't biting."

For a variety of reasons, ranging from bass predation to bait sellers to water level changes, Crane Prairie's once abundant leech population is greatly reduced. The chub population has declined, too, as have the dragonfly nymphs. But other trout forage is doing well, such as damselflies, *Callibaetis*, and midges. This is just one example of how a lake's fishing environment can shift. The trout are aware of these changes and adapt to them. Anglers should do the same.

Still-fishing has always been popular in Crane Prairie. Power Bait, nightcrawlers, dragonfly nymphs (erroneously called "hellgrammites" by many) are all effective. Bait-fishing from the bottom up works well, although in some areas it is very easy to get tangled in downed timber. Fishing from the top down works, too, but use the smallest bobber you can get away with. These fish can be pretty subtle, so you need something that will signal the slightest action on your bait.

Trollers do well here, but mostly in the early season. Later, the water level drops and the weeds grow, making trolling rigs gather more vegetation than trout. Common lures to troll are Woolly Buggers, Crane Prairie Specials, and various spinners and spoons. As mentioned before, the chub population is down, so trolling chub imitations is not as effective as it once was.

Crane Prairie is Mecca for many fly-anglers. Its prolific hatches, clear waters, and big, wily trout challenge the skills of experts. And there aren't many waters in the world where you can cast a dry fly and have some hope that a ten-pound rainbow might suck it down.

This lake is noted for its massive *Callibaetis* hatches. These start in late spring and continue through summer, then taper off in fall. In spring, the duns are size 12 or 14 and get progressively smaller and lighter through summer, ending at about size 18. A spring hatch of Crane Prairie *Callibaetis*, with five to ten-pound rainbows grabbing duns everywhere you look, is a sight to make any angler's eyes go wide with excitement. Float tubers fishing these hatches will often unconsciously draw their legs up close to their body, as if one of the big rainbows might mistake a foot for a *Callibaetis* dun.

The *Callibaetis* hatches can occur throughout the lake and usually start at midday. Take advantage of pre-hatch activity by fishing a good nymph pattern, such as a Flashback Pheasant Tail, subsurface on an intermediate line beginning a couple of hours before the expected hatch.

Damselflies are another major hatch at Crane Prairie. The nymphs can be fished all season, but prime time is during pre-hatch migrations beginning late June and continuing through July. The nymphs travel in hoards from weed beds to above-water objects like standing timber. Position yourself near such an object, cast out, and retrieve back toward it. Crane Prairie's big trout seem to prefer a sparse damselfly pattern retrieved right along the weed tops. A slow retrieve is usually best—the slower the better.

Damsel nymphs can be a good choice even during a *Callibaetis* hatch. Trout hovering near the bottom waiting for *Callibaetis* duns to appear on the surface will sometimes take a well-presented damsel

A Crane Prairie rainbow comes to the boat before being released.

nymph as a target of opportunity.

Midges are also common in Crane Prairie, and are often the most important trout food in September and October. Channel areas such as Rock Creek can be prime as large schools of lunker trout cruise around devouring midges as they emerge at midday. There are three ways to imitate these hatches: pupa on the surface, pupa fished deep, and hatching midge. I believe the latter two are the most effective. See Chapter 6 for more information on fishing midge hatches.

Other important patterns to carry are leeches, caddis, and scuds. A leech fished near dawn and dusk in areas of downed timber can be effective.

Fly-fishing leaders for Crane Prairie should be long and tapered to as fine a tippet as you feel you can get away with. When the big trout are active, 4X is a good choice for surface flies, and you might get away with 3X subsurface. You have to make a trade-off between hooking a fish and the potential for losing it. When I fly-fish here, I use at least a 12 foot leader, and often go to 15 feet or more. The long leader seems to help.

Beginning anglers often have an irresistible urge to carry a big trout to the resort so they can have a Polaroid taken of them holding their dead trophy. Before you are tempted to do this, think for just a moment. It took three to five years to grow that fish, and you can kill it in three to five minutes. The big fish are not especially good eating. If left in the lake, they will grow larger and provide sport for others, including you. Isn't that a better legacy than a blurred and faded photo?

**Fishing Regulations.** Open from the fourth Saturday in April to October 31. Up to five trout per day may be kept, with a six-inch minimum. Only one trout over 20 inches may be kept. Up to five bass per day may be kept, with no more than three over 15 inches. There is no limit on whitefish. Closed to angling one hour after sunset to one hour before sunrise; this is the general rule throughout Oregon for trout, but in Crane Prairie it applies to all fish, including bass. All tributaries to Crane Prairie are closed to angling after August 31.

**Boating Regulations.** 10 mph speed limit.

# Crescent Lake

Size: 3,600 acres    Elevation: 4,850 feet

Kokanee and mackinaw provide the major fishing action at Crescent Lake. Rainbow and brown trout are also available, but not in the numbers and size they once were. Crescent Lake boasts a resort, five campgrounds, and three picnic areas, so vacationers are well provided for. One of the campgrounds is for groups, and another is a horse camp; reservations are required for both of them.

Crescent Lake is a natural lake, but a dam was built to raise the water level. Water is drawn off for irrigation throughout the summer, so the lake can drop as much as fifteen feet by season's end. The water here is deep and clear, and while that clearness adds to the lake's beauty, it indicates that it is not as productive for fish as some other lakes. Like other large lakes in this area, Crescent Lake can have its share of wind, and boaters should keep their eyes on the weather.

Inflow to the lake is limited to Summit Creek, Windy Creek, and a few intermittent streams. Crescent Creek is the primary outflow; it feeds into the Little Deschutes River.

The lake is near Highway 58, so it is easily reached from major population areas.

**Access**. Turn where there is a sign on Highway 58 for "Crescent Lake/Campgrounds/Resort-Marina." This puts you onto road 60, which is paved. After 2.2 miles you reach a junction; there is a message board here (Crescent Lake has a lot of message boards; it must be a hard place to meet people). Turn right to continue on road 60 and reach the northwest shore, or go straight on road 6015 to reach the resort and Simax Beach.

After a short distance, road 6015 turns right. A quarter mile later you reach another junction. Go left to reach Simax Beach (there is a sign) in less than a half mile, or go straight to get to the resort.

Road 60 skirts the northwest shore, but for the first three-and-a-half miles it is too far from the lake for reasonable access. This part of the shore has homes on Forest Service leases, and the area should be treated as private property. After the summer homes, road 60 closely follows the shore, and there is good access to the lake for a couple of miles. The Tranquil Cove and Tandy Bay picnic areas are on this stretch of the road.

After the Tandy Bay Picnic Area, the road stays well back from the lake, but spur roads give access to Spring Campground (road 6000-230) and Contorta Point Campground (6000-280). Road 60 becomes gravel at the turn-off to Spring Campground, and veers away from the lake area after the turn-off to Contorta Point.

In Crescent Lake's clear waters, you can fish for mackinaw, kokanee, and rainbow trout.

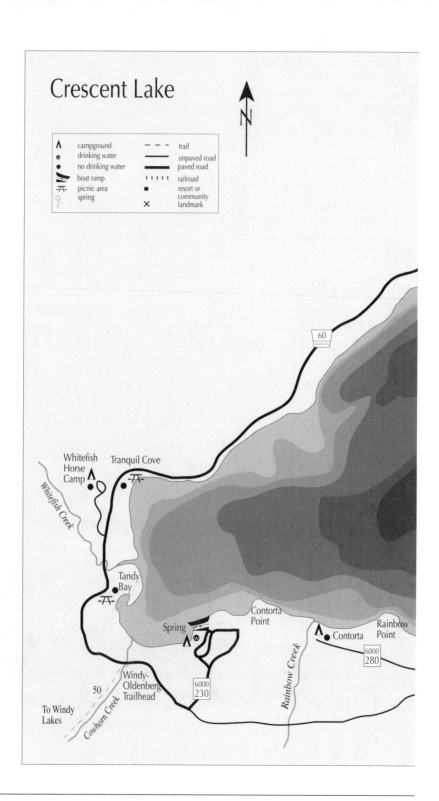

# Crescent Lake

N

| | | | |
|---|---|---|---|
| Λ | campground | – – – | trail |
| ⊕ | drinking water | —— | unpaved road |
| ● | no drinking water | ━━ | paved road |
| ⛵ | boat ramp | ∎∎∎∎∎ | railroad |
| 🔀 | picnic area | ∎ | resort or community |
| ⚲ | spring | × | community landmark |

Whitefish Creek

Whitefish Horse Camp

Tranquil Cove

60

Tandy Bay

Spring

Contorta Point

Rainbow Point

Contorta

6000 280

Rainbow Creek

Windy-Oldenberg Trailhead

50

6000 230

To Windy Lakes

Cowhorn Creek

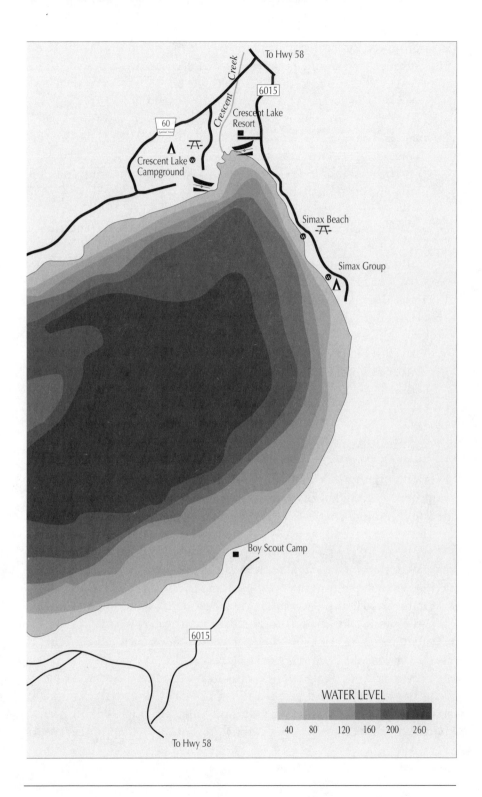

To Hwy 58

6015

Crescent Creek

Crescent Lake Resort

60

Crescent Lake Campground

Simax Beach

Simax Group

Boy Scout Camp

6015

To Hwy 58

WATER LEVEL

40    80    120    160    200    260

**Campgrounds, Recreation Sites, and Services.** In addition to the store at the resort, there are a gas station, stores, RV park, restaurants, and a motel on Highway 58 near the turn-off to the lake.

*Crescent Lake Resort.* The original resort was built in 1927, and updated a few times since then. You can reach the resort at 503-433-2505. The mailing address is PO Box 73, Crescent Lake, OR 97425. Resort services include:

> 15 cabins from $55 per night, with a two night minimum; all cabins have kitchens
>
> Recreation area and snack bar in the lodge; hours are 11-7
>
> Store with sundries, limited groceries, and tackle (no flies); hours are 8-5
>
> Boat and motor, canoe, and pedal boat rental
>
> Moorage

*Simax Bay Picnic Area.* The beach here is wide and sandy, with a gentle slope into the water that makes it a good family swimming spot. You have a nice view of the lake and surrounding mountains. Facilities are tables, fire pits, drinking water, and pit toilets.

*Simax Group Area.* This area has undergone new construction and is scheduled to open in 1995 with camping areas for three different groups. To make a reservation, call the Crescent Ranger District at 503-433-2234.

*Crescent Lake Campground.* The turn-off from road 60 has a sign. You enter on road 6000-180, a paved road that ends at the campground in about a quarter mile. This is a pleasant campground set among tall evergreens on a hill above the lake. There are 46 designated sites, including three tent-only sites (36-38). A message board is located near the turn-off from road 60.

There are two paved boat ramps here, one for high water and one for low. Both ramps have a dock. A large trailer parking lot is back up the hill about a quarter mile from the ramps.

On the road to the low water ramp, there are two pull-outs for handicapped visitors. Day-use picnic tables are nearby up a short dirt hill.

A day-use area is located near the spillway next to the boat ramp. It has two tables and a fire pit. A pit toilet is nearby.

*Tranquil Cove Picnic Area.* This day-use area off road 60 has a broad hard-packed sand beach and is popular with boaters. There are tables, fire pits, trash dumpsters, and pit toilets, but no drinking water. There is not a boat ramp, but under dry conditions it is possible to launch a trailered boat from the beach.

*Whitefish Horse Camp.* There is a sign on road 60 for this camp-ground, which is not on the lakeshore. A gravel road leads into camp. There are 19 designated sites, three with four wooden horse corrals and the rest with two horse corrals. Wooden gates are provided with the corrals. Stock water is available. Drinking water is not available now, but may be in the future. Each camp site has a table and fire pit, and pit toilets are available. Reservations are recommended; call the Crescent Ranger District at 503-433-2234. A trail leads from the camp to the Windy-Oldenberg trail (see Chapter 3).

*Tandy Bay Picnic Area.* This day-use area offers a picnic table and a pit toilet. It is just off road 60 near the lake. A trail leads to the beach, but lake access is not as convenient as at Tranquil Cove.

*Windy-Oldenberg Trailhead.* Road 6000-250 is a gravel loop that goes to this trailhead. There is a pit toilet here, but no other facilities. From here you can reach Windy Lakes (four-and-a-half miles) and the Summit Lake Trail (four miles); see Chapter 3 for details.

*Spring Campground.* The turn-off is signed on road 60. A message board is located at this junction. The campground is a half mile down the paved road (6000-260). Sixty-eight designated sites are scattered among lodge pole pines.

The concrete boat ramp has a dock, and adequate trailer parking is available above the ramp. The ramp may be closed in low water.

A picnic area near the lake offers a nice view of the mountains. Drinking water, tables, and pit toilets are provided.

*Contorta Point.* Turn off road 60 onto 6000-280. There is a message board at this junction. The campground begins about a half mile down the dirt road. The road forks at the beginning of the camping area; there is another message board here. Turn left into one camping area, or continue a quarter mile to the end of the road (almost) where there are more sites.

This is a primitive campground, without water or trash pickup. Dust is a problem due to the dirt roads. There are pit toilets at both camping areas. Only the area near the end of the road has tables; it also has better access to the lake. Neither area has fire pits or a boat ramp. There is no fee for camping here.

**How to Fish Crescent Lake.** The drought years have been hard on Crescent Lake and have had an impact on the fishing. The lake is one of the first to be drawn down for irrigation, and drought means that it gets

Crescent Lake is a natural body of water, but a dam was added to raise the water level. Draw-downs for irrigation can affect the fishing.

drained more than usual and fills up less. The result has been low water levels for several years, and even after 1993's heavy snowfall and wet spring, the lake was back down to drought levels by August.

Kokanee, which provide 80% of the fishing action on the lake, have not been able to spawn in their usual places. ODFW has tried to make up for this by doubling their kokanee stocking. It is hoped that a string of wet winters will bring the lake back up to its former productivity. Anglers will have to be alert to changing fishing conditions and adjust their tactics.

The Crescent Lake kokanee usually divide into two groups, one that is mostly fish under 11 inches, and the other made up of 12-20 inch fish. These schools travel the lake between Simax Beach, the island in Tandy Bay, and Crescent Creek. Some years they seem to start at Simax, and other years at the island. In either case, they end the season near Crescent Creek, where they would spawn if they could reach the stream.

Normal kokanee techniques work well here. If you don't want to hunt all over the lake for the kokanee, check with the resort to find where and at what depth they are being caught. Early season is best, with a definite slump in mid-July and August.

Kokanee provide dinner to successful anglers, but they are also the main meal for the lake's big mackinaw. During the good years of the past, Crescent Lake anglers would annually net hundreds of mackinaw over 20 pounds. However, mackinaw fishing declined substantially during the drought years. The reason for this is not clear. Were there fewer mackinaw? Or were they just harder to catch? It is possible that the latter is true.

A reason for this may be the extra kokanee that ODFW stocked; perhaps the mackinaw have had so many small fish to dine on that they have no motive to grab an angler's lure. Perhaps they are all sitting on the bottom burping and complaining about heartburn, and as soon as Crescent Lake comes back to normal the mackinaw will go on a rampage, smashing plugs with gay abandon. Let's hope so.

Like the kokanee, the mackinaw tend to divide into two groups. There are those that follow the kokanee around; they can usually be found in front of the summer homes on the north shore. The others can be found in the deep water between the Scout camp and Contorta Point. Both areas produce about the same number of fish, but the latter area produces bigger ones.

Kokanee are the primary forage fish for Crescent's mackinaw, and kokanee-looking lures are the most popular with mackinaw anglers. The techniques discussed in Chapter 7 work well here. The big macks can be hooked on fly gear when they are near the surface after ice-out (if the lake freezes). One place to try is around Contorta Point, where there is some good structure for the macks.

Rainbow and brown trout fishing used to be good at Crescent Lake, with brown trout up to 10 pounds and rainbow well over six. But again, the drought has taken a toll on the fishing. Fingerlings are still planted in the lake, but the frequent water-level changes have devastated the shallow littoral habitat vital to good trout fishing.

Rainbows are still around, and, unlike Odell Lake, Crescent has several shallows where they can be caught by bank anglers. Some good areas are the northwest shore where the road comes back to the lake, and near the campgrounds at the west end. Simax Beach is also a good area to try, if you don't get too deep.

**Fishing Regulations.** Open from the fourth Saturday in April to October 31. Up to five trout per day may be kept, with a six-inch minimum. No more than one trout over 20 inches may be kept. There is no limit on whitefish.

**Boating Regulations.** There are no special boating regulations.

# Cultus Lake

Size: 785 acres    Elevation: 4,650 feet

Cultus Lake is a medium-sized lake of great depth. Along with Odell and Crescent Lakes, it provides mackinaw fishing for Cascade Lakes anglers. Stocked rainbow trout are also available, but mackinaw are the primary quarry.

The Chinook word "cultus" means "disgustingly worthless," even "vile" or "evil." Few anglers would agree that the word applies to this lake, however. The shore is heavily forested, and while there are no views of snow-capped peaks, this is still a pretty place to fish. Because it is much smaller than the other two mackinaw lakes in the area, it has an intimate feel and is more easily comprehended.

The major outflow from the lake is Cultus Creek, which drains into Crane Prairie Reservoir. Inflow is from Winopee Creek, which comes down from a chain of high lakes north of Cultus Lake. There are also several underground springs that feed the lake. The water level does not change much over the summer.

There is no speed limit here, and the surface water temperature warms to the 60s in summer. For these reasons, the lake is popular with water skiers beginning in July. The remainder of the summer, high speed boats trolling water-skiers often outnumber very slow speed mackinaw anglers trolling Flatfish. Windsurfers also find the lake desirable.

**Access.** This is a high snowfall area, and the road to the lake is often blocked until mid-May.

From road 46, take road 4635 (paved) where there is a sign for Cultus Lake Resort. There is a message board here. After 1.6 miles you come to a junction; turn left for the resort or continue straight for the campground. On the way to the campground, you pass the picnic area. After the campground turn-off, the road becomes gravel until it reaches the Winopee Lake trailhead. The trailhead is as far as vehicles with trailers should go because turn-around space is limited beyond there. The road turns to dirt and continues another quarter mile before ending.

The Winopee Lake trail follows the north shore of Cultus Lake for a couple of miles, wanders away from it, and comes back again near West Cultus Lake Campground, which can be reached only by boat, bike, or on foot. This campground can also be reached by a trail that heads at

4630-640 near Little Cultus Lake, then continues past Deer Lake to the campground. There are two other camping areas that can only be reached by boat or foot. One is about a mile from the Winopee Lake trailhead, and the other is about a mile further.

**Campgrounds, Recreation Sites, and Services.**

*Cultus Lake Resort.* The resort is open from mid-May to mid-October. The mailing address is PO Box 262, Bend, OR 97709. Phone is 503-389-3230. Resort services include:

- 23 cabins from $45 per night; all but five have kitchens
- Restaurant with large patio overlooking the lake and swimming beach; open 8 AM to 8 PM
- Store with sundries, limited groceries, and tackle, including a good selection of flies
- Boat and motor, rowboat, canoe, kayak, windsurfer, and Hobie Cat rentals
- Moorage for cabin guests (only)
- Gas and propane
- Swimming beach for guests
- Emergency phone

These anglers had a good morning of mackinaw fishing in Cultus Lake. Rainbow trout are also available.

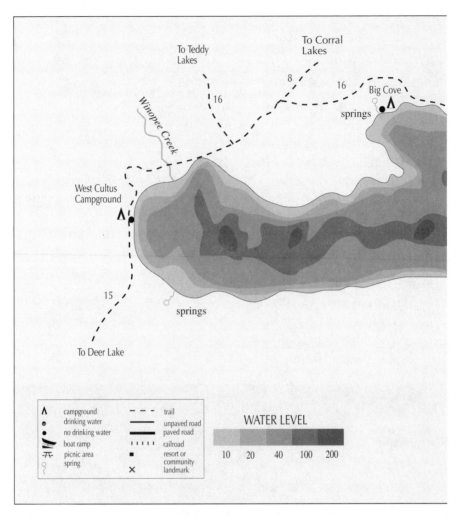

To Teddy
Lakes

To Corral
Lakes

8

16

16

Big Cove

springs

Winopee Creek

West Cultus
Campground

15

springs

To Deer Lake

| Λ | campground | – – – | trail |
| ⊕ | drinking water | —— | unpaved road |
| ● | no drinking water | ━━ | paved road |
| ⇒ | boat ramp | ıılıı | railroad |
| ⅄ | picnic area | ■ | resort or |
| ⚲ | spring | | community |
| | | | landmark |
| | | ✕ | |

WATER LEVEL

10   20   40   100   200

*Cultus Lake Picnic Area.* Before you reach the campground you pass a picnic area set among tall pines and firs. There are pull-outs on both sides of the road for parking. The picnic area has tables, barbecues, pit toilets, and changing rooms for swimmers. Drinking water is nearby at the campground. The beach is mixed sand and pea gravel, and there are large logs to sit on for those who would rather watch a swimmer than be one. No dogs on the beach, please.

*Cultus Lake Campground.* There are 54 designated sites in the campground. A unique feature is an amphitheater that is used for nature talks and similar events.

The paved boat ramp is at the entry to the campground; it has a

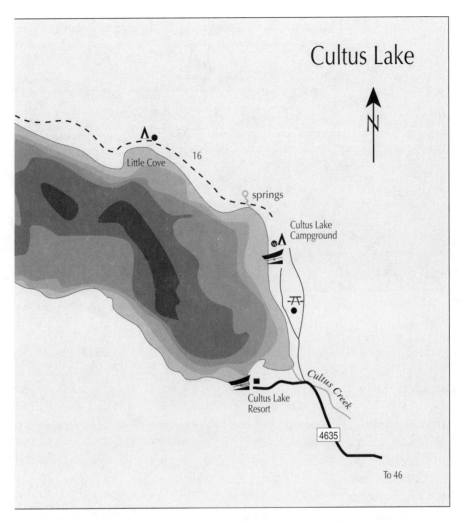

Cultus Lake

Little Cove

16

springs

Cultus Lake
Campground

Cultus Lake
Resort

Cultus Creek

4635

To 46

N

dock. This can be a busy place, so be prepared and keep your loading and unloading to 10 minutes or less. Trailers may be parked in the area, but there is a fee to keep one there overnight.

*Big Cove and Little Cove Camps.* You can only get to these by boat, bike, or foot. Little Cove is about a mile from the Winopee Lake trailhead, and Big Cove is about a mile further. Both are on protected bays. The beaches are sandy and the bottoms slope gently away, making these popular spots for swimmers. Composting pit toilets are provided, but there are no tables, fire pits, or drinking water. Pack out all your trash. There are no boat docks here, and the shallow bays may cause problems for some boaters who need to beach their craft overnight.

Cultus Lake has three camps that can only be reached by boat. This one is West Cultus.

*West Cultus Lake Camp.* This camp can be reached only by boat, bike, or by foot; see the section above on access. The campground is spread out along the west shore, with many good tent sites in the trees. Because it is at the west end of the lake, this campground is protected from the wind. There are tables, fire pits, and pit toilets, but there are no drinking water or trash pickup. There are two docks for boats, and the sandy shore is suitable for beaching boats. While the beach is good here, the bottom drops off quickly so it is not as good for swimming as the Big Cove and Little Cove camps.

**How To Fish Cultus Lake.** Cultus Lake does not have as many big mackinaw as Odell and Crescent lakes, and the typical Cultus mack weighs between three and seven pounds. However, they are as eager here as anywhere, and 15 pound fish are available.

The primary forage fish in this lake is whitefish. This is different than the other two mackinaw lakes, where kokanee make up much of the diet.

The west end of the lake is shallower than the east end; most mackinaw anglers avoid these ends of the lake and focus on the middle half. There is an area of rocky cliffs along the north shore. Rocky structure abounds in this area, and you can fish fairly close to the cliffs. Be careful, though; that structure is good fish habitat, but it can grab the gear of unwary anglers. A good trolling strategy is to work the area between these cliffs and about two-thirds of the way to the opposite shore. The north shore between Cultus Lake Campground and Big Cove Campground can also be productive.

Rainbow trout habitat is limited at Cultus Lake, so angling for them is primarily a put-and-take fishery for hatchery fish. ODFW stocks the lake through June. By July, most of these are gone, but there are always a few that make it until fall. Few hatchery fish will survive the winter, however.

The primary trout food is midges, but there is so little for the poor rainbows to eat that they are not fussy, eagerly pursuing anything with a remote resemblance to food. Fish the shallow margins, such as the areas near Cultus Creek, Big Cove Campground, and some of the south shore, especially at the west end. Also, the coves off the rocky northwest shore can hold receptive fish.

Fishing from the top down is the best bait-fishing strategy here; otherwise you will either be too deep or will hang up in a tangle of underwater logs. Fly-fishing can be productive, especially if you use midge patterns near dusk; the rest of the day, cast damselfly nymphs or Woolly Buggers near shore. Small spinners are also a good approach in these areas.

**Fishing Regulations.** Open from the fourth Saturday in April to October 31. Up to five trout per day may be kept, with a six-inch minimum. No more than one trout over 20 inches may be kept.

**Boating Regulations.** There are no special boating regulations.

# Davis Lake

Size: 3,000 acres    Elevation: 4,400 feet

The first time I visited Davis lake, I stood on the east bank of the Odell Creek channel at dusk and watched big rainbows gorge on tiny midges on the surface. First, I'd see a trout's back break the surface, then its dorsal fin, and last the tail would disappear. There was a lot of space between the dorsal fin and the tail; these were the biggest rainbows I'd ever seen, most of them between 18 and 26 inches. People in Bend could hear me panting.

Unfortunately, this was early in my fly-fishing career, and I didn't know how to recognize a midge hatch, let alone fish it properly. I hooked one trout on a small Elk Hair Caddis and soon lost it. On other trips I experienced massive *Callibaetis* hatches in the main body of the lake. Again, trout averaging 22 inches rose frequently to suck down *Callibaetis* duns.

Years later, after seven years of drought, I stood in that same place on the Odell channel. Odell Creek was a trickle. Where there once had been a lake, now there was only dried mud. There were no midges. The extensive weed beds had dried out. The trout were gone.

During the drought, Davis Lake suffered more than any of the other Cascade Lakes. A lake of over four square miles was reduced to the size of a large stock pond. It was devastated, nuked beyond recognition.

The problem is that Davis Lake leaks. It was formed about 3,000 years ago by a lava dam that blocked Odell Creek, and the dam is very porous. In addition, this is a shallow lake with extensive surface area, so a lot of water is lost to evaporation. It takes a steady inflow from Odell Creek to keep ahead of water loss.

Because Davis Lake is shallow, it is not good for still-fishing. Because it is weedy, it is not good for trolling. For these reasons, Davis Lake was designated as fly-fishing-only water in 1939, and has kept that status for all but five years since.

The wet winter of 1992-1993 refilled the lake to within a couple of feet of its optimal level, and ODFW is restocking it. But it takes more than water and a truck load of fingerlings to restore a lake; the entire aquatic food chain needs to re-establish itself. I don't know how long that will take, or to what state Davis Lake will return. I hope we get some more wet winters and the lake returns to its former greatness. Soon.

**Access**. Road 46 passes the east side of Davis Lake, but not close enough for access to it. A well-signed turn-off at the junction of 46 and 62 sends you a quarter mile down a paved road that "T"s into a gravel road. A right turn puts you onto 4600-850, which proceeds 2.0 miles north and ends at the lava flow. The campground and boat ramp are off this road. Road 4600-850 makes a tight loop between the start of the campground and the lava flow.

Turning left (south) at the "T" puts you onto 4600-855, which goes 2.2 miles to East Davis Lake Campground. The campground is down a spur road off 4600-855; there is a sign.

Roads 4600-850 and 4600-855 are close to the lake, and spur roads

Large and shallow, Davis Lake nourishes trophy rainbows for fly-fishers.

take you to primitive, no-amenities camp sites. However, except at the main campgrounds, fishing access from these roads is poor due to the extensive marsh and reed areas between the shore and the main body of water.

You can get to the west side of the lake on road 4660, a two-lane gravel road that takes off from road 46 three-and-a-half miles south of the lake, and comes back to 46 near Wickiup Reservoir. From this road, you can turn onto 4669 (there is a sign) and go 1.7 miles into West Davis Campground. Another dirt spur, road 4660-600, goes from 4660 to East Davis Campground.

Beyond its turn-offs to the campgrounds, road 4660 stays near the lake. There are quite a few rough dirt spurs that head off this road towards the lake, but none reach it. They all end either too far from the lake or near the lake but with extensive reedy areas blocking easy access to the water. None of these roads is useful for fishing access.

Besides road access, there is a pleasant half-mile trail between the West Davis and East Davis campgrounds.

**Campgrounds and Recreation Sites.** As discussed in the section on access to the lake, people sometimes camp in areas other than the established campgrounds described below.

*Lava Flow Campground.* This is a beautiful camping area set in tall ponderosa pines near the lava dam that created Davis Lake. It is well-

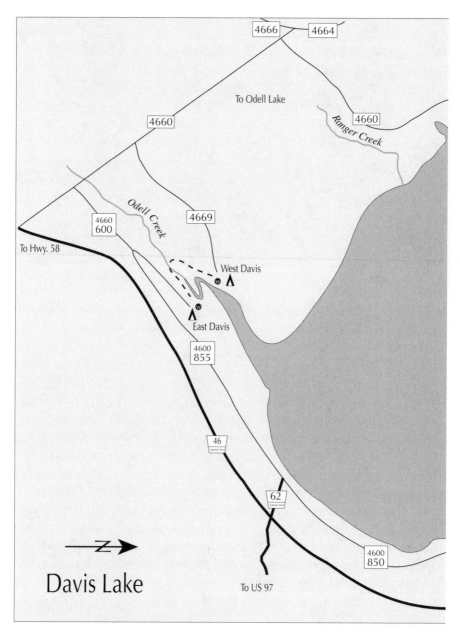

To Odell Lake

Ranger Creek

4666    4664

4660        4660

Odell Creek

4660
600

4669

To Hwy. 58

West Davis

East Davis

4600
855

46

62

4600
850

Davis Lake

To US 97

suited to those seeking escape from crowds and "civilization," but be warned that it is a primitive camping area with limited facilities. There are camp sites at the south end where you enter the campground, and again at the north end by the lava dam. The southern area has tables, drinking water, a concrete boat ramp, and pit toilets. Trash dumpsters

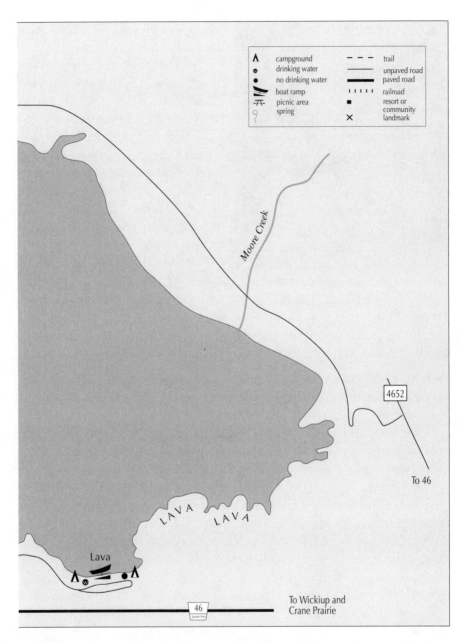

are absent, however, so pack out your garbage. The northern end is similar, but has no boat ramp or drinking water. There is no fee .

*East Davis Lake Campground.* The twin campgrounds of East Davis and West Davis are on the banks of Odell Creek where it enters the lake. They are separated by only 250 yards of open space, but are a half mile

Lava Flow Campground backs right up to the lava dam that created Davis Lake.

apart by trail and five miles apart by road.

East Davis is a full-service campground with 33 designated sites. There is a message board at the entrance. Camp sites are well-spaced for privacy, and some are along Odell Creek. Be prepared for mosquitoes. There is a rough dirt boat ramp into Odell Creek near the fence line. From it you can reach the lake except in times of low water.

*West Davis Lake Camp-ground.* This is a full-service campground similar to East Davis. There are 21 designated sites. There is no boat ramp, but it is possible to launch a canoe or other small craft from the bank, and sometimes the shore is dried out enough to back a trailer down.

**How to Fish Davis Lake.** It's hard to say what is the right strategy for Davis Lake since it is in transition. Therefore, this section describes fishing as it used to be, with the hope that it will soon be that way again.

One thing to keep in mind is that in the early stages of the lake's revival, the stocked trout will be small and aggressive. As they mature (if allowed to do so) they will become more picky and wary.

In the past, trout would be well scattered throughout the lake in spring, but the northeast end near the lava dam was a reliable place to fish. A good angler casting leeches could pick up a trout every hour or so. That's not a lot of fish, but each one would be four or five pounds. Damselflies could also be productive on the lake.

As summer progressed and the water warmed, trout would migrate towards the cooler water of the Odell Creek channel. *Callibaetis* and midge hatches were the rule, with the former occurring at midday, and the latter mostly at dusk. At these times, there would be a steady flow through the channel, so it was more like fishing a river than a lake.

Leaders needed to be long (12 feet or more) and tapered to at least 4X, with 5X better for hooking but not for landing. Never be afraid of small flies with big fish. A size 18 or 20 midge pupa tied on a stout nymph hook is sufficient to land big trout like these, if the angler is careful.

**Fishing Regulations.** Fly-angling only. Open from the fourth Saturday in April to October 31. Two trout per day may be kept, with a six-inch minimum. There is no limit on whitefish. No angling from a motorboat while the motor is operating. In order to protect spawning rainbows, Odell Creek is closed until June 1 from Odell Lake to the ODFW markers at Davis Lake.

**Boating Regulations.** 10 mph speed limit; see above for regulations about fishing from a motorboat.

# Devils Lake

Size: 23 Acres     Elevation: 5,440 feet

I don't know why this pretty little lake with its turquoise water should be named as it is. Perhaps the name comes from one of the inlets, Hell Creek. One September I measured the temperature of this stream at 39 degrees, so apparently it is the creek from which they derived the expression "cold as Hell." When the creeks are flowing, the lake can be quite chilly (in the mid to low forties); for a float tuber, that's a real fanny freezer.

The lake holds stocked rainbow trout of 8-11 inches. They are catchable all summer. There are also a few stunted brook trout that reproduce naturally in the lake.

Devils Lake is eminently accessible, with road 46 skirting two sides, and a trail around the rest. A tent-only campground is on the west side. It is a good lake for canoes, kayaks, and float tubes, however you will soon run out of nooks and crannies to explore. The maximum depth is nine feet.

**Access.** Road 46 passes very near the north and west sides of Devils Lake, using the lake like at pylon to make a sharp 90-degree turn. Along the north side there are two large turn-outs for parking cars. A float tube could be launched from here, or, if you are athletic and motivated, a canoe could be put into the water.

Access to the west side of the lake is from the campground. There is a sign on 46 for "Wickiup Plains/Trailhead/Devils Lake CG" that points you to it. This is a major trailhead, serving hikers and mountain climbers bound for South Sister or the Pacific Crest Trail.

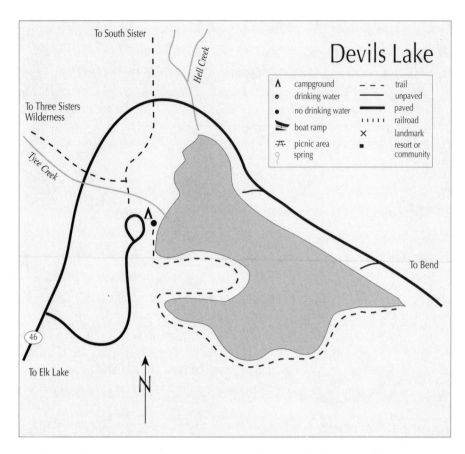

From the campground, you can take a trail that goes around the south end of the lake. Thus, the entire lakeshore is reachable.

This is a heavy winter area, and the road may not open until after Memorial Day.

**Camping and Recreation Sites.** Devils Lake Campground is very small, consisting of six tent-only sites. Each site has a table and fire pit; pit toilets are available. There are no drinking water or trash dumpsters here, and no fee.

There are also some good dispersed camp sites along the trail around the south shore.

**How to Fish Devils Lake.** This is not a difficult lake to fish. There are very few weeds for fish to hide in, and the shallow depth and clear water make every fish visible. The west end of the lake is all shoal area, and much of it is less than three feet deep. However, unless the lake is warm, you can find fish in this shallow water as well as in the "depths" of the east end.

The lake can heat up in summer if the inlet streams are low. When the water warms, the fish will head for the east end where it is deeper. The eastern-most turnout on 46 can be used for bank fishing in the deeper water of the lake.

These trout are not fussy or sophisticated. There isn't much food for them, so they are eager for anything that looks close to edible. On the other hand, because the water is so clear, you should use thin leaders or tippets (two to four pound for bait-fishing, 5X or 6X for fly-fishing). These fish aren't going to tax your gear.

The primary foods are midges and a few mayflies. The shallow depth, clarity, and hungry trout mean that bait, lures, and flies can be fished at almost any depth with equal success. Fly-fishers may find this a good place to use dries; the clear water makes each take visible, which adds to the pleasure.

**Fishing Regulations.** Open from the fourth Saturday in April to October 31. Up to 10 trout per day may be kept, with a six-inch minimum. No more than five trout over 12 inches, and no more than two over 20 inches.

**Boating Regulations.** No motors allowed.

Tyee Creek is one of two inlet streams at the shallow west end of Devils Lake.

# East Lake

Size: 1,028 acres    Elevation: 6,380 feet

East Lake has been a favorite with anglers since it was first stocked with trout in the late 19th century. Today it offers rainbow trout fishing and the chance to catch a trophy-sized brown trout. Recent stockings of kokanee and Atlantic salmon will, if successful, increase the diversity of the fishery. An abundant chub population provides forage for the larger game fish in the lake.

East Lake and its neighbor Paulina Lake were once one body of water; see the section on Paulina Lake for the geologic history of the two lakes. Like Paulina, East Lake has subsurface geothermal springs. There are no inlets or outlets, but some water seeps through the lava and reaches Paulina Lake.

East Lake is a better rainbow fishery than Paulina Lake because it has more vegetated shoal areas. There used to be a brook trout fishery here, but stocking has ceased and it is a rare event to hook a brook.

A resort and three campgrounds serve visitors. Travelers to East Lake need to be prepared for the weather, which ranges between warm and balmy, and windy and cold. A few years ago, the resort ran out of ice on the Fourth of July. The next Fourth of July it snowed.

East Lake is easily reached on a paved road. Because it is so high, the fishing season opens later here than at other lakes in the region.

**Access.** Road 21 heads east from US 97, 22 miles south of Bend and 6 miles north of La Pine. A sign on US 97 directs you to East and Paulina Lakes. It's a rough climate up here, and snow often delays the opening of the road until Memorial Day. A major road maintenance project, complete in 1994, gives road 21 a new surface, so its rough and multi-patched past will live only in memory—for a few years, anyway.

The first point of road access is at East Lake Campground, about 17 miles from the junction with US 97. After this campground, road 21 is back from the lake for about a mile, then touches it again at Hot Springs Campground and stays close until the resort. For most of the distance between Hot Springs and the resort, there is access to the lake shore. Past the resort, a road continues into Cinder Hill Campground, then ends.

Unlike Paulina Lake, East Lake has no trail around the shore. However, it is possible to walk along the shore from Cinder Hill

Big brown trout sometimes cruise near the rock cliffs of East Lake's east shore.

Campground to the resort. From the resort to East Lake Campground there are some high banks, and walking is difficult. It is an easy walk from East Lake Campground to the White Pumice Slide, and there is a rough trail above the high-water line. After the White Pumice Slide, walking gets more difficult. By the time you reach the Red Fissure, you have to be highly motivated (and possibly deranged) to continue walking. The cliff area is impassable unless you want to go over the top of them (not recommended!).

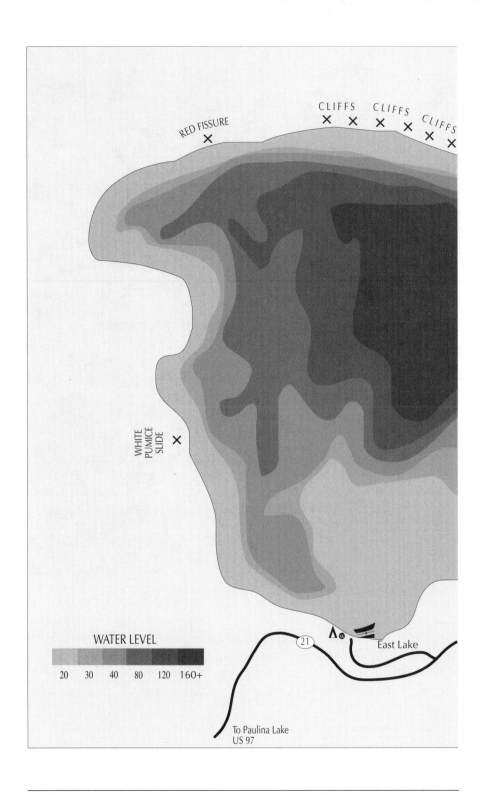

RED FISSURE
×

CLIFFS  CLIFFS  CLIFFS
×  ×  ×  ×  ×
×  ×

WHITE
PUMICE
SLIDE  ×

WATER LEVEL

20   30   40   80   120  160+

21

Λ 𝔀

East Lake

To Paulina Lake
US 97

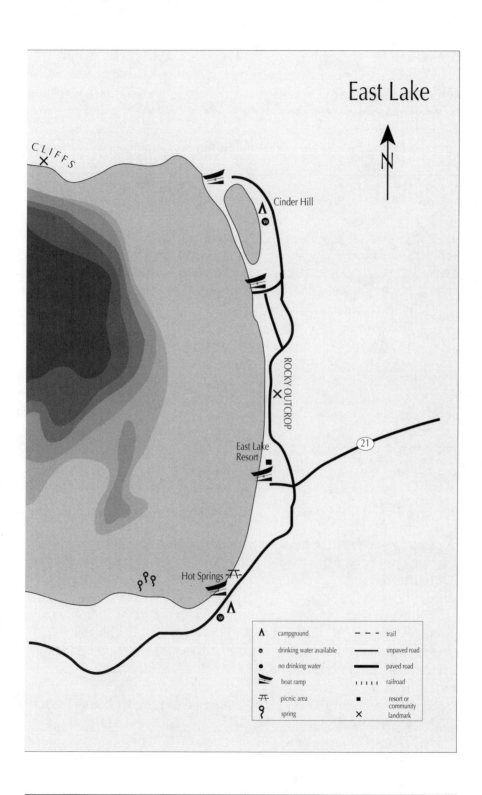

East Lake

N

CLIFFS ✗

Cinder Hill
Λ
ⓦ

ROCKY OUTCROP
✗

East Lake
Resort
■

21

Hot Springs 🔆
♀♀♀
Λ
ⓦ

| | | | |
|---|---|---|---|
| Λ | campground | – – – | trail |
| ⓦ | drinking water available | —— | unpaved road |
| ● | no drinking water | ━━ | paved road |
| 🚤 | boat ramp | ıııııı | railroad |
| 🔆 | picnic area | ■ | resort or community |
| ♀ | spring | ✗ | landmark |

**Campgrounds, Recreation Sites, and Services.** At this time, fees for the Forest Service campgrounds are paid at a booth on road 21 several miles before the lake. There are several campgrounds on road 21 before you get to the lakes area, but they are not described here because they are too far from the fishing.

*East Lake Resort.* The resort has been serving anglers since the 1920s, and many old and ardent anglers started their fishing careers here as youngsters. Stop here and ogle the two mounted brown trout that resort owner John Hofferd bagged in September 1992. That should stoke the fires of angling desire!

The resort closes in mid-October, but the cafe closes in mid-September. The resort's phone number is 503-536-2230. Mail can be sent to PO Box 95, La Pine, OR 97739. Facilities include:

> Eleven cabins with kitchens, from $58 per night
>
> Playground area for children
>
> Full-hookup RV park; $12 per night
>
> Store and cafe with sundries, limited groceries, and tackle (the only flies are Teeny nymphs and leeches); hours: M 9-2, T-closed, W-F 9-2, S-S 8-2 and 5-8
>
> Boat and motor, rowboat, and paddleboat rental
>
> Boat ramp
>
> Fish cleaning station in middle of cabin area
>
> Fishing guide service
>
> Coin-operated showers and laundromat at the RV park; open to the public
>
> Gas and propane
>
> Pay phones

*East Lake Campground.* The campground is a short distance down a paved spur road from road 21. There are 29 designated camp sites. Both flush and pit toilets are provided, and some of the toilets are suitable for the handicapped.

The boat ramp is paved, but in low water the pavement does not reach the lake, and the last few feet are on coarse sand. The beach here is wide, and many boaters beach their craft overnight, tying-up to large stakes pounded into the sand. There is ample trailer parking space above the ramp.

There is a rather barren day-use area near the boat launch. It has four tables and two barbecues. Water and pit toilets are nearby.

*Hot Springs Campground.* No; there are no hot springs at this camp-

East Lake's campgrounds have good places to beach a boat overnight. Because wind and waves can be strong, many boaters pull their craft onto the sand and tie them to stakes.

ground. The "hot springs" are underwater thermal vents nearby in the lake. The campground area is on the south side of road 21, so there are no lake-side camp sites. Forty-three designated sites are provided with the usual Forest Service amenities.

The paved boat ramp is across the road from the camping area and has a dock and a large trailer parking area.

There is a day-use area next to the boat ramp. Facilities include tables, barbecues, and pit toilets.

*Cinder Hill Campground.* This is the camp at the end of the road, about a half mile past the resort. It is large and spread out, with 109 designated sites. Both flush and pit toilets are available. The road is paved, so dust is minimal.

There are two paved boat ramps. Only the one at the south end has a dock. There are beaches near each ramp for those who want to leave their boat overnight.

There is a day-use area near each boat ramp, but only the north one has tables and barbecues.

**How to Fish East Lake.** All fish in East Lake are stocked, with the exception of some naturally reproducing brook trout. ODFW puts in over 100,000 rainbow fingerlings each year, but only 10,000 brown trout.

This means that the brown trout are not as plentiful, but grow to a larger size.

The tui chub (roach) population provides forage for the brown trout and larger rainbows. If anglers release the Atlantic salmon so they can grow to around 16 inches, they will prey on the chub as well, and East Lake will be able to apply more of its resources to growing trout.

East Lake was once noted for its large rainbows, but in recent years these have not been present. The reasons for this are not clear.

Unlike its neighbor Paulina, East Lake has quite a bit of vegetated shoal area, and most fish are taken there. The southern half and eastern quarter of the lake are under 50 feet deep. The rest of the shoreline drops off steeply, but the margins can still offer good fishing for those pursuing trout with lures and flies. There are abundant weed beds in front of the resort, and trolling outside them can be productive.

The hot springs are a good bet in early season. When you first troll through the hot springs area, you might wonder just what exactly was in that sausage your fishing partner ate for breakfast. Don't blame your companion. It's the hot springs; the smell gives them away. This is a good place to start because the water is warmer and fish are drawn to it. However, don't get trapped into thinking this is the only place to find early season fish. The first time I visited East Lake, all the anglers were trolling through the hot springs area. I soon tired of the bustle and let my boat drift with the wind while I cast a spinner. I had more action that way than I could get fishing with the crowds.

As the water warms, the fish spread out and go deeper. Some good areas for bait-fishing are:

*Off the White Pumice Slide*, stay within 200 feet of shore or you get into water that is too deep.

*Near the point* at East Lake Campground.

*In front of the resort,* about a third of the way across the lake.

*Near shore* between the rock cliffs and Cinder Hill Campground.

Still-fishing from the bottom up is effective in these areas. The primary catch will be rainbows, but the occasional lunker brown has been known to grab a gob of Power Bait. When still-fishing, don't get too deep. You won't find many trout feeding below 30 feet.

East Lake is not as clear as its neighbor Paulina, but you should still use leaders of about four-pound test, and two-pound is even better when bait-fishing. When trolling, keep your leader at least four feet long, and go up to six or eight feet if you are fishing in the middle of a bright sunny day.

Trollers generally work around the margins of the lake, using lures with a yellowish cast to imitate the chub. When trolling in front of the resort, get as close as you can to the weed beds without hanging up.

The northern half of the lake is quite deep. The break to deep water is about in the middle and is a prime place to find fish. You can fish this break by trolling between the White Pumice Slide and a rocky outcropping between the resort and Cinder Hill Campground.

Fly-fishers can do well in all the margins and still-fishing areas. There are hatches of *Callibaetis*, as well as frequent morning and evening midge hatches. Damselfly nymphs are always a good choice in early season, and the weed beds in front of the resort are a promising place to cast them. The Atlantic salmon are partial to all the same flies as the rainbows. Muddler Minnows work well for them, too.

Fly-fishers should stick to 5X tippets on leaders of nine feet or longer. You might go to 4X or 3X if you are after lunker browns subsurface, but recognize that you are trading off fewer strikes for holding power.

Streamer flies and lures with a yellow cast have worked well in the past because they resemble the colors of the chub that the brown trout forage on. But the recent introduction of kokanee may cause the browns to expand their diet. Therefore, you should also carry lures and flies that are black (or dark blue) on top with a silvery body. Over the next few years, these may prove quite effective on East Lake.

If you are after brown trout, read the "how to" section for Paulina Lake. Most of what is said there applies to East Lake as well, except East does not have Paulina's rocky coves. In East Lake, the prime brown trout areas are shoals next to drop-offs and ledges.

East Lake gets a lot of wind, even more than Paulina. Brown trout anglers can use that wind to advantage. Baitfish are pushed into shoal areas by high winds, and big browns move in and feed on them. So fishing windward shores when the lake is choppy can be a good brown trout strategy.

**Fishing Regulations.** Open from the Saturday prior to Memorial Day weekend to October 31. Up to five trout per day may be kept, with a six-inch minimum. Only one fish over 20 inches may be kept.

**Boating Regulations.** 10 mph speed limit.

# Elk Lake

Size 250 acres    Elevation: 4,900 feet

Elk Lake is a scenic lake with a large population of small kokanee and brook trout. The lake is lightly used by anglers and is more popular with sailors and windsurfers. The Cascade Lakes Highway (road 46) passes down the west side, and access is excellent. This is a civilized lake, offering a resort, three campgrounds, and two picnic areas.

Like its neighbors, the Lava Lakes and Hosmer Lake, Elk Lake was created by lava dams from Mt. Bachelor flows. Other than snow melt, there is little surface inflow to the lake, but subsurface springs at the north and northwest shores add water. There is no outlet other than seepage through the lava. Much of the lake is shallow, although it has a maximum depth over 60 feet near the south end.

This is a pleasant lake, large enough to have variety, yet small enough to explore in a day. Winds are reliable, but the wave action is not high. The powerboat speed limit is ten mph. For these reasons the lake has long been attractive to sailors. More recently, windsurfers have discovered it.

Swimming is also an attraction here, and there are well-developed beaches for bathers. The water temperature can hit the high sixties in summer, which makes for good swimming, if not good fishing.

Because Elk Lake is in a heavy snow area, it may open late. Some anglers are tempted to push the season and fish through the ice in the spring. This is a dangerous idea because the ice is often rotten by that time, and it is very easy to fall through.

**Access.** Elk Lake has excellent road access. Road 46 skirts the western shore, while road 4625, a two-lane gravel road for most of its length, goes around the north and east sides. Only the south end is inaccessible by road. The north end of 4625 joins 46 where there is a sign for "Sunset View." There is a sign for "Hosmer Lake/E. Elk Lake" on road 46 where the south end of 4625 comes in. From there, you continue past Hosmer Lake and reach Elk Lake at Little Fawn Campground.

In addition to the resort in the northwest corner of the lake, there are two campgrounds and a picnic area off 46, and one campground and one picnic area off 4625. Most of the north and northeast parts of the lake have cabins along the shore. These are on Forest Service leases and must be regarded as private property. Do not drive down the roads to

Reliable winds combine with scenery to make Elk Lake popular with sailors. Do they know how many brook trout are under their keels?

the cabins, walk through the property, or come ashore on their beaches.

### Campgrounds, Recreation Sites, and Services.

*Elk Lake Resort.* There is a sign for the resort on road 46. The main building for the resort is an old log lodge, and if you don't duck your head when you go in you will become closely acquainted with one of the old logs. The resort can be reached at PO Box 789/Bend OR 97709, or through the Bend mobile operator at YP73954 (Call the operator, ask for "Bend mobile operator." Give the number to the mobile operator; $3.50 charge). For fishing purposes, the resort closes in mid-September. Services include:

> Twelve cabins, all but two with kitchen; from $58 per night
> Breakfast and lunch counter
> Restaurant for dinner; reservations are required
> A few supplies, snacks, and sundries
> Boat with motor and canoe rentals by the hour or day
> Moorage by the day or month
> Boat ramp
> Emergency phone

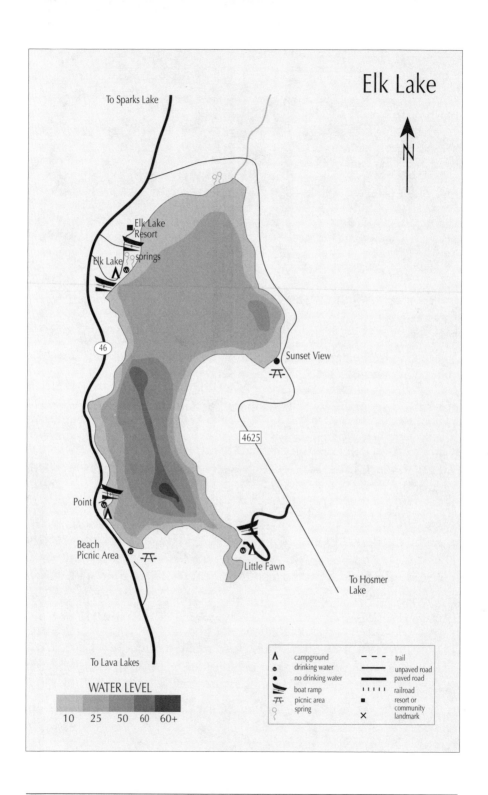

Elk Lake

To Sparks Lake

N

Elk Lake Resort

springs

Elk Lake

46

Sunset View

4625

Point

Beach
Picnic Area

Little Fawn

To Hosmer
Lake

To Lava Lakes

WATER LEVEL

10   25   50   60   60+

Λ     campground                    - - -   trail
⊕     drinking water                         unpaved road
●     no drinking water                      paved road
      boat ramp                    ı ı ı ı ı   railroad
⊼     picnic area                    ■       resort or
⸮     spring                        ×        community
                                             landmark

*Elk Lake Campground.* This popular campground is reached from a spur road just south of the turn-off for the resort; there is a sign. This is a full-service campground, with water, pit toilets, trash dumpsters, and a paved boat ramp. Trailer parking is very limited.

There are 22 designated camp sites, each of which has a table and fire pit. A fee is charged. The camp sites are rather close together, and really level sites can be hard to find.

*Point Campground.* This is a small shoreside campground similar to the one near the resort. There is a sign on 46 pointing to the campground. Camping is in nine designated sites. Sites are close together and sandwiched between the lake and road 46, so daytime traffic noise can be distracting. There is a boat ramp.

*Beach Picnic Area.* Road 4600-488 leads to this day-use area. There is no sign at the turn-off, but warning signs are placed about a half mile before. A pleasant sandy beach offers swimming and gorgeous views of South Sister and Broken Top. There are pit toilets, water, tables, and barbecues, but no boat ramp.

*Little Fawn Campground.* Turn off 4625 onto 4625-500. The campground is 0.4 miles down a paved road. It is on a pleasant little cove on Elk Lake's eastern shore. There is a sandy beach for swimming (6 AM to 9 PM), and a day-use area is nearby. The water is shallow here, so the beach is well-suited to youngsters. However, more serious swimmers may be happier up the road at Sunset View.

A concrete boat ramp is down a rough dirt road. Turn-around is extremely limited, and this is not a very useful ramp.

Camping is in 20 designated sites. Drinking water is available from a pump. There is a separate area for groups; call the Bend Ranger District at 503-388-5664 for reservations.

*Sunset View Picnic Area.* Turn off 4625 onto a gravel road that soon ends at the picnic area. There is no overnight use at this site, but the swimming and picnicking are great, and it is a popular place for families and wind surfers. The beach and lake bottom are coarse sand, and the bottom slopes gently from the shore. The water can be "bracing," but refreshing. There are tables with barbecues, pit toilets, and a changing hut for swimmers. Drinking water is not available, and there is no boat ramp.

**How to fish Elk Lake.** Elk Lake is like two different lakes joined together. Most of the north half of Elk Lake is shallow, around ten feet deep.

There is a depression over 25 feet deep in the west corner in front of Sunset View picnic area. A subsurface spring is at the north end of the lake, and there is another between the resort and the campground. The south half of the lake is much deeper, with a maximum depth over 60 feet off Point Campground. Most of the shore is rocky, and weed growth is minimal.

ODFW stocks brook trout every year. The typical fish is between ten and fifteen inches, with an occasional fish over 20 inches. That's not bad for brook trout. The fish can be found throughout the lake, usually near the shore. Like most brook trout fisheries, angling is best in early season, rolls off in mid-summer, and picks up again in fall.

Most brook trout are taken by still-fishers using worms off the bottom. However, fly-fishers can do well here. There is a large crayfish population, and the brookies eat them. Therefore, a crayfish pattern (see Chapter 6) or brown Woolly Bugger fished near the bottom can be an effective tactic. Check out the small coves and points; these can be prime collecting places for trout.

Trollers and casters can also catch trout here. Locals feel that lures with a gold tint work best.

Kokanee are the other species in the lake. In relation to their food supply, there are too many of them, and that is why the bag limit is so

Elk Lake has several scenic picnic areas and swimming beaches.

high (25 fish per day). ODFW would be delighted if you frequently took home your daily bag limit. There are just too many fish, and they mature at a small size (under ten inches).

Kokanee are concentrated in a small area known as "Kokanee Hole." It is about 100 feet in diameter and is near Point Campground in the deep water. You can locate yourself by lining up between a road culvert that comes out from under road 46 just north of Point Campground, and a barren rocky patch on the opposite shore. Since the fishing is in such a small zone, jigging a small lure is a good bet (see Chapter 7).

**Fishing Regulations.** Open from the fourth Saturday in April to October 31. Up to 10 trout per day may be kept, with a six-inch minimum. No more than five trout over 12 inches, and no more than two over 20 inches. Up to 25 kokanee per day with no size limit. Kokanee limits are in addition to trout limits.

**Boating Regulations.** 10 mph speed limit.

# Hosmer Lake

Size: 160 acres    Elevation: 4,950 feet

Hosmer Lake is a fly-fishing-only lake with trophy brook trout and landlocked Atlantic salmon. Fly-fishers travel from all over the Northwest to fish here. The lake is also popular with bird watchers, who come to view its rich and varied avian population, and with canoeists, who appreciate a large, calm body of water. The area has an abundance of other wildlife, including deer, elk, raccoons, and otter. And mosquitoes.

Mt. Bachelor dominates the east side of the lake, while South Sister and Broken Top offer breath-taking views to the north. With all these natural wonders and great fishing, it's hard to believe that the lake's original name was Mud Lake, and it once hosted a thriving population of carp.

Lava flows dammed Quinn Creek and created the lake. There is no outlet, but water seeps into the lava dam and disappears underground. Hosmer is a shallow lake, and the extensive weed growth indicates that it is well on its way to becoming a meadow. In the meantime, there is some excellent fishing.

Hosmer feels like two lakes joined by a marshy, weed-choked channel. Quinn Creek flows into the northern part, which is quite shallow and cold. The southern part is warmer and deeper.

Birds enjoy Hosmer Lake as much as fly-fishers. Early in the season it can be hard to sleep because of the ruckus the birds make. I recall one June when I was awakened about 3:30 AM by a bittern's loud and frequent "!Cung !GA Chunk!" Several others started in, and were soon joined by the entire avian chorus. I never did get back to sleep. Still, it's better than traffic noise and police sirens.

This is a heavy snow area, so the lake can open as late as Memorial Day. One year, though, cars couldn't get in until mid-June.

**Access.** There is a sign for "Hosmer Lake/E. Elk Lake" on road 46 which directs you onto road 4625, which is paved. After 1.1 miles you come to the turn-off for the boat ramp.

From the boat ramp area, you can turn left into South Campground. That road leads eventually to Mallard Marsh Campground.

If you continued on 4625 past the boat ramp turn-off (4625-600), there is another turn-off in about 200 yards that leads to both campgrounds. At this point 4625 becomes two-lane gravel and continues up the east side of Elk Lake, eventually joining road 46.

Alternatively, you can come from the north end of Elk Lake on 4625, beginning where it intersects 46 at the north end of Elk Lake. At that intersection, there is a sign for "Sunset View Picnic Area."

Most people reach the lake from the boat ramp. There is a rough trail around the south end of the lake from the boat ramp, but access to the water is very difficult because of heavy reed growth.

Mallard Marsh Campground has a trail that leads to a canoe and float tube launching point in the middle of the channel; this trail is between camp sites 14 and 15. Although it can be a messy kick or paddle through shallow water to reach the main channel, this trail saves a lot of work in the summer when fishing is concentrated in the channel area. The alternative is a long trip from the boat ramp.

There is another trail at Mallard Marsh Campground. It heads off just past camp site 15 and goes along the lake shore for a ways, then angles back past Peel Pond and returns to the campground. The length is about one mile, and it is a pleasant walk with views of South Sister, Broken Top, and the north end of the lake. However, the shore area is thick with reeds, and there is poor fishing access.

Wide marshes and reeds line the lake and make it impossible to fish from the bank. Without some kind of watercraft you can't fish Hosmer.

Hosmer Lake sits in the shadow of Mt. Bachelor and is popular with canoeists as well as fly-fishers.

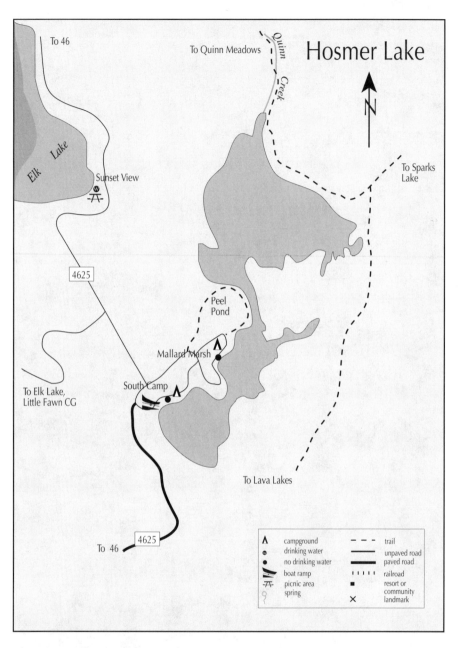

**Hosmer Lake**

To 46

To Quinn Meadows

Quinn Creek

To Sparks Lake

Elk Lake

Sunset View

4625

Peel Pond

Mallard Marsh

South Camp

To Elk Lake, Little Fawn CG

To Lava Lakes

To 46    4625

| | | | |
|---|---|---|---|
| Λ | campground | - - - | trail |
| ⊙ | drinking water | —— | unpaved road |
| ● | no drinking water | ▬▬ | paved road |
| | boat ramp | ׀ ׀ ׀ ׀ | railroad |
| ⅄ | picnic area | ■ | resort or community landmark |
| | spring | ✕ | |

**Campgrounds and Recreation Sites.** Most people who camp at Hosmer Lake are either fly-fishers or bird watchers, so they tend to be earnest, well-behaved organic people who go to bed early instead of having loud drunken parties. Both campgrounds are primitive, lacking drinking water and trash dumpsters. Nevertheless, they are popular and fill up quickly, usually starting on Thursdays.

*South Campground.* The campground starts near the boat ramp and is set near the lake shore among tall trees that offer shade. The road is dirt and is dusty in dry weather, so drive very slowly through the campground. A few sites are near the lake and have a view. Bring mosquito repellent.

Camping is in 23 designated sites that are well separated from each other. Pit toilets are provided. Each camp site has a table and fire pit, but there are no drinking water or trash dumpsters. There is no fee.

The boat ramp is paved and has a large parking area.

*Mallard Marsh Campground.* This campground is almost identical to South Campground. There is no boat ramp, but you are not far from the one at the south end of the lake. As you might expect from the name, bring mosquito repellent. Camping is in 15 designated sites, each of which has a table and fire pit. There are pit toilets, but no trash dumpsters or drinking water, and no fee. There is a campground host here who can provide you with information on Hosmer's fishing and natural history.

**How to Fish Hosmer Lake.** There is little natural reproduction in Hosmer; all of the Atlantic salmon and most of the brook trout are from hatchery stockings. The brookies are typically 12-18 inches, with an occasional fish reaching five pounds. The population seems to be doing well, and ODFW feels it would be a good thing for the fishing if anglers took a few brook trout for the frying pan.

The Atlantic salmon are stocked at 8-10 inches. The typical catch is 14-18 inches, with a few fish over 20 inches. The Atlantics were first stocked in 1958, and for many years this was the only lake west of the Mississippi where they were established. The strain of fish was changed some years ago. The earlier Atlantics were very surface-oriented, which made for great dry fly sport. They were good sport (and eating) for osprey, too, and were soon decimated. The current strain is not as large nor as oriented to surface flies.

Over the last several years, the fishery at Hosmer has changed. The balance seems to have shifted to favor the brook trout, and they are the most abundant fish.

Like most brook trout fisheries, Hosmer is best early in the season. At this time of year, most of the fish are in the south end (where the boat

FLY FISHING ONLY
WITH FLY ROD FLY REEL AND FLY LINE
NO SPIN OR FIXED SPOOL REELS ANY
TYPE BACKING LINE AND BARBLESS FLY
RELEASE ALL ATLANTIC SALMON

HOSMER LAKE →
BOAT RAMP →
SOUTH CG. →
← MALLARD MARSH CG.

Hosmer is a fly-fishing-only lake.

ramp is) because the water is warmer. As the season progresses, they migrate to the channels to take advantage of Quinn Creek's cool inflows. At the height of summer, it is possible to catch a few fish in the north part of the lake, although most people don't go up there except to explore. As fall approaches and the water cools, fish migrate back toward the south end.

Within these migration patterns, all of the water can be productive. The margins near the weeds are especially so, but don't ignore the middle of the lake in the morning and evening when midges are hatching. A slow, near-surface retrieve of a midge pupa of appropriate size and color can be effective for Atlantics at this time. When not actively rising, the brook trout seem to stay deeper than the Atlantics, and you should carry a sinking line to get down to them.

Hosmer is a great producer of damselflies, *Callibaetis*, and midges. Leech patterns also produce, and you might try a crayfish imitation as well. Late July-early August is when many damsels return to lay eggs. A blue Braided Butt Damsel dry fly can entice large fish to make slashing surface strikes; if that doesn't get your juices flowing, take up another sport!

*Callibaetis* hatches are usually midday, occurring for a couple of hours sometime between noon and 5:00 PM. Dries can be effective during the hatch, but don't forget to start fishing the nymphs near the weed beds beginning a couple of hours before the hatch (see Chapter 6). In May, the *Callibaetis* are about a size 14, but by the end of summer smaller duns of about size 18 (and lighter in color) are the norm.

There are also occasional hatches of caddisflies. See Chapter 6 for patterns and tactics.

I would mislead you if I didn't say that Hosmer can be tough. The fish here are not dummies. They see a lot of anglers all season long, so you need to approach the fish quietly and stealthily, and fish a well-tied fly that imitates real food.

One of the keys to fishing Hosmer is distance: between you and the fish, achieved with a long cast; between the fly-line and the fly, achieved with a long leader (12 foot minimum, 15 foot is better). Use fine tippets, preferably 6X. Like I said, Hosmer can be tough.

During the summer, many fish pack into the narrow channel and are easily seen. A steady stream of canoes, rowboats, and float tubes pass through here, and its hard to resist a few casts at such obvious (and large) trout. How many times a day do you think the fish see this parade?

A plump brook trout cruises the rich weed beds of Hosmer Lake.

How dumb do you think they are? You may be more productive staying away from the concentration of fish (and water craft) and plying quieter waters. Also, you will be much more productive in the channel when the light is low, either at the beginning or end of the day, or on overcast days.

Every now and then a poacher comes into Hosmer thinking he can get away with a spinning rod and a nightcrawler. So what if all those wimpy fly-fishers yell at him? Big deal; there's not a phone for 25 miles, so who's going to call the cops? Well, one guy took that approach a while back. He didn't know that the camp host has a radio. By the time the poacher got to the boat ramp with a few dead Atlantic salmon in his boat, the State Police were waiting and wrote him a ticket with a hefty fine.

**Fishing Regulations.** Open from the fourth Saturday in April to October 31. Fly-angling only (a spinning rod with a casting bubble is not fly-angling) with barbless hooks. All Atlantic salmon must be released unharmed, but two brook trout per day may be kept if they are longer than six inches. You may not fish from a motor-propelled craft while the motor is operating.

**Boating Regulations.** No motors allowed except electric motors. 10 mph speed limit. See the fishing regulations above for rules about fishing from a motor-propelled craft.

# Lava Lake

Size: 350 acres    Elevation: 4,790 feet

Lava Lake is a productive fishery for brook and rainbow trout. The scenery is spectacular, with fine views of South Sister, Broken Top, and Mt. Bachelor. Services at the lake include a resort, an RV park, and a campground.

The lake was created by a lava dam from Mt. Bachelor flows. There are no inlet streams, but water seeps in from Wire Meadow and from springs in the northeast corner of the lake. In normal years Lava Lake has no outlet, but water is lost through the lava. The lake level can vary several feet over the season, and, contrary to intuition, the highest levels are in late summer.

This is a popular lake with anglers. It is accessible, not difficult to fish, and reasonably productive for 10-14 inch trout, with some over 16 inches. Every year a few trout over six pounds are taken.

At one time Lava Lake was overrun with chub, to the point that the trout fishery was seriously depleted. However, for the last several years the resort owners have made a huge effort to eliminate as many chub as possible. Each year, tons of chub are netted, killed, and removed from the lake. The results have been outstanding, and the trout have responded well to the reduction in competition.

**Access.** Signs on road 46 point to "Lava Lake Resort." Road 4600-500 takes you 0.9 paved miles to the resort, campground, and boat ramp. There is a turn-off that leads to Little Lava Lake; a message board is located at this fork.

A trail goes around the east side of the lake. It begins close to the lake at its southern end, and offers good access to the lake for bank anglers fishing off the rocks. The trail continues to Sparks Lake near road 46. Several trails come together near Lava Lake, so follow the signs carefully.

Another trail begins in the same area and goes about a quarter mile to Little Lava Lake.

Parts of the southwestern shore can be reached from an unsigned trail that heads west from the resort. Because of heavy reed growth there is no access to the lake for the first quarter mile. After that, however, access is excellent. The trail proceeds to Wire Meadow, a boggy and buggy place except in late season. This trail is a good choice for bank

Beautiful scenery and bountiful rainbows—that's Lava Lake.

anglers. It is also used by float tubers to reach the south and west shores without having to kick over from the resort area.

**Camping, Recreation Sites, and Services.**

*Lava Lake Resort.* The resort is at the end of road 4600-500. While it does not offer cabins, it does have a full-hookup RV park with 24 spaces. Rates for the RV park start at $14 per day, with weekly rates available. Call 503-382-9443 or 503-382-7857 for reservations. The mailing address is PO Box 989, Bend, OR 97709.

Resort hours are 7 AM to 8 PM every day until after Labor Day, when they are reduced. The resort stays open until the end of October, but may shut down earlier if the weather turns snowy. In addition to the RV park, services include:

      Store with supplies, sundries, and tackle, including flies
      Boat and motor, rowboat, canoe, and paddleboat rentals
      Boat moorage on daily or weekly basis
      Fishing tackle rental
      Showers and laundromat

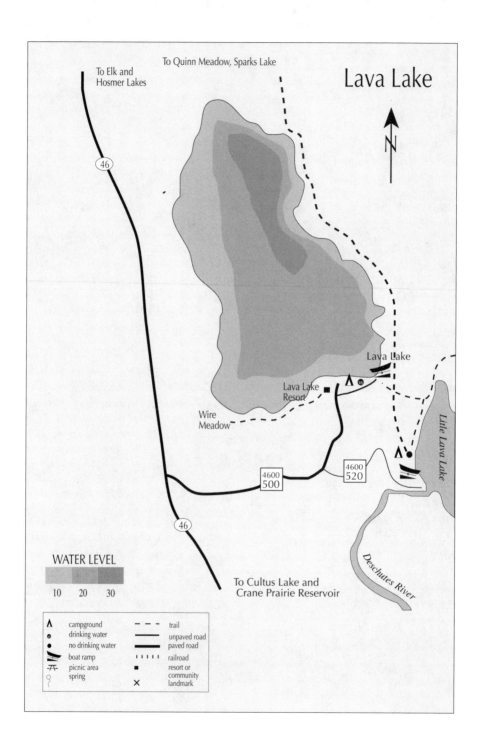

Lava Lake

To Quinn Meadow, Sparks Lake

To Elk and
Hosmer Lakes

46

N

Lava Lake

Lava Lake
Resort

Wire
Meadow

Litle Lava Lake

4600
500

4600
520

46

Deschutes River

WATER LEVEL

10    20    30

To Cultus Lake and
Crane Prairie Reservoir

Λ    campground
ⓦ    drinking water
●    no drinking water
⊵    boat ramp
⊼    picnic area
ⓢ    spring

- - -    trail
———    unpaved road
━━━    paved road
ı ı ı ı ı    railroad
■    resort or
      community
✕    landmark

Holding tank dump station
Gas and propane
Emergency phone

*Lava Lake Campground.* This campground is near the resort on road 500. The concrete boat ramp is near the fish cleaning station. The ramp has a dock, and there is a small area on which boats may be beached. Adequate trailer parking is near the ramp.

The usual Forest Service amenities are provided to 44 designated sites. A day-use area is located between the resort and the campground.

**How to Fish Lava Lake.** Lava Lake is not a difficult lake to fish, but it can be moody. When it's good, it can be really good, and when it's slow you'd swear the fish moved to another county.

All parts of the lake can have good fishing, often on the same day. When the water warms, however, trout tend to move to the deeper water along the eastern edge. There is a point on the northeast shore known locally as "Velveeta Point." Trout congregate off here in hot weather because the water is deep and subsurface springs pump in cold water.

The west side offers shallow weedy water that is good for fly-fishing, but fly-fishers should not limit themselves to this part of the lake, especially if they carry sinking lines. The northwest shore is a good spot for evening fishing because it is soon shaded.

There is no part of the lake that is unproductive, although the margins are generally the best. When fishing Lava Lake, try several places, and don't get rooted to one spot. The lake is large enough to be interesting, but not so large as to be intimidating or unknowable. It can easily be explored in a day's fishing.

Still-fishing is the most popular tactic on the lake, with Power Bait preferred. Although most still-fishers gather at Velveeta Point, all areas can produce for a knowledgeable angler, especially in cooler weather.

Trollers can do well, as can casters and fly-fishers. In one afternoon on the lake I caught fish on bait, spinners, spoons, flies, and plugs. They all worked well when fished at the proper depth.

Presenting your offering at the right depth is especially important here. The lake is shallow enough to enable good growth of aquatic vegetation, but deep enough to offer cover to the trout. Fish will find a favored temperature/oxygen/cover depth and cruise there. If you are fishing bait off the bottom in 30 feet of water, and most of the trout are

The resort at Lava Lake offers tackle, boat rentals, and a full-hookup RV park.

cruising at 20 feet, you may have a slow day.

Experiment with different depths until you find what works best. With bait fished from the top down, you can adjust the length of leader below the bobber. With bait fished from the bottom up, park your boat over different depths. If casting, try different count-downs so you cover a range.

This is a fairly clear lake, so four-pound leaders or less are the rule for still-fishers. Fly-anglers should stick to 5X tippets for surface flies, but can use 4X if fishing subsurface. The lake has good hatches of *Callibaetis*, usually occurring between 10 AM and 1 PM, as well as midges and caddis. Leeches and damselflies are also present.

Lava Lake is stocked with two strains of rainbows. One strain comes from the Oak Springs hatchery, as do most of the other stocked rainbows in the Cascade Lakes. The other strain originated in Klamath Lake and is being stocked on an experimental basis. The Klamath Lake strain is believed to be more apt to eat other fish. The lake still has a few chub, and these new rainbows may feed on them. Thus, fly-fishers may want to try some streamer patterns that imitate baitfish, and trollers may want to pull some plugs such as black and gold Jensen Minnows or Rapalas. This is just one example of how a fishery can change due to a variety of factors, and why anglers need to be alert and adaptable. Norman and Roberta LaFleur, who have fished Lava Lake all summer for years, told me that they have never seen it the same two years in a row.

**Fishing Regulations.** Open from the fourth Saturday in April to October 31. Up to five trout per day may be kept, with a six-inch minimum. Only one trout over 20 inches may be kept.

**Boating Regulations.** 10 mph maximum speed.

# Little Cultus Lake

Size: 175 acres    Elevation: 4,750 feet

Little Cultus is a small lake, very shallow in some areas and quite deep in others. It is a brook trout fishery, although an occasional rainbow trout can be found. The lake is modestly productive and not heavily used. Facilities are limited and primitive.

The lake is surrounded by large trees that come right down to the shore. Over the years, many trees have fallen into the lake, where they provide habitat for aquatic life and hiding places for fish.

**Access.** From road 46 take road 4635 (paved) where there is a sign for "Cultus Lake." After 0.7 miles, turn left onto 4630, which is gravel. You reach a "T" in 1.7 miles. Here, road 4630 goes to the left, but you continue straight; there is a sign. You are now on road 4636, which reaches the lake in 0.7 miles.

When you arrive at the lake, there is a fork. Go left on 4636 to the campground and boat ramp. The right fork goes to Deer Lake. Road 4636 continues to the Lemish Lake Trailhead and Irish and Taylor Lakes. After the boat ramp, it stays away from Little Cultus, but there is a spur that leads to a camping area near the west end of the lake.

The right fork at the east end of the lake is road 4636-640, a rough gravel and dirt road that skirts the north shore of the lake for a while. There are several no-amenity camp sites along the road near its beginning. At the end of this road (1.7 miles) you can park and walk a short distance to Deer Lake. This trail continues past Deer Lake to the West Cultus Campground and Cultus Lake.

**Campgrounds and Recreation Sites.** Little Cultus Lake Campground is a primitive facility with limited amenities and no fee. Camp sites are wherever you make them along 4636 near the lake. A few tables are scattered around, and there are drinking water and pit toilets, but no trash dumpsters. Dust is a problem due to the dirt road through the campground.

The concrete boat ramp is a quarter mile past the start of the campground; follow the signs and have faith. There is limited parking and turn-around for those with trailers.

There is another camping area past the boat ramp. Take road 4636-600, and you will reach a primitive area with a couple of tables (period).

**How to Fish Little Cultus Lake.** ODFW stocks around 10,000 brook trout fingerlings here each year. Most of the trout you catch will be about 10 inches, but occasionally a larger fish is picked up. Like most brook trout lakes, the best times to fish Little Cultus are early in the season, September, and October. Early season has the heaviest fishing pressure, but this can be a nice, uncrowded lake to fish at the end of the year.

There are a few rainbow trout in the lake. They are naturally reproducing, but most of them are smaller than the brook trout.

The lake basin is of glacial origin. It is shallow on the east end, but has a very deep hole in the west.

Trolling is popular here, and is done mostly in the west end to avoid

Little Cultus Lake is small and off the beaten path, but it holds a few surprises.

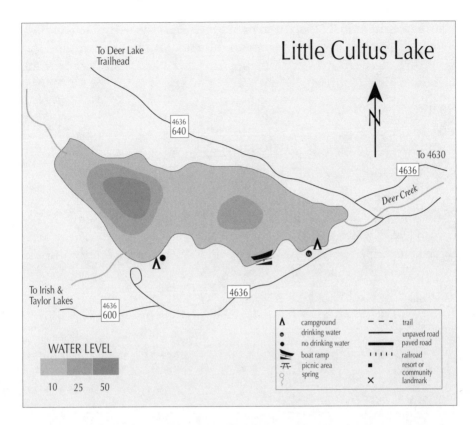

Little Cultus Lake

To Deer Lake Trailhead

4636 640

N

To 4630

4636

Deer Creek

To Irish & Taylor Lakes

4636 600

4636

| ⋀ | campground | - - - | trail |
| ⦿ | drinking water | ——— | unpaved road |
| ● | no drinking water | ▬▬ | paved road |
| ► | boat ramp | ı ı ı ı ı | railroad |
| 🎋 | picnic area | ▪ | resort or |
| ⚲ | spring | | community |
| | | × | landmark |

WATER LEVEL

10   25   50

shallows and weedy areas. But this tactic misses the interesting water. Little Cultus has one of the most intriguing and varied bottom structures of any of the Cascade Lakes. It is sometimes rocky, sometimes weedy, and sometimes silty. There are shoals and holes in close proximity, and sudden changes in depth. The bathymetric chart shown here, and any verbal descriptions, are inadequate. This lake structure has many surprises for anglers who have the patience and skill to probe it.

I think the best way to explore Little Cultus is from a float tube or an anchored boat. Poke around and cast flies or spinners into the holes and pockets, and see what they yield. The lake is small and shore access is good, so a float tuber won't have to kick very far.

The primary fish foods are damselfly nymphs, *Callibaetis* mayflies, and midges.

Bank-fishing is also an option if you pick a place where you can cast to water that is 10-15 feet deep. If you use bait, you are probably better off fishing from the top down.

**Fishing Regulations.** Open from the fourth Saturday in April to October 31. Up to 10 trout per day may be kept, with a six-inch minimum. No more than five trout over 12 inches, and no more than two over 20 inches.

**Boating Regulations.** 10 mph speed limit.

# Little Lava Lake

Size: 110 acres    Elevation: 4,750 feet

Little Lava Lake is a small, quiet lake with primitive facilities. It is more famous as the source of the Deschutes River than for its fishing, but it can still be a good alternative to more crowded arenas. ODFW stocks the lake every other year with 15,000 rainbow trout fingerlings. Brook trout are occasionally stocked, as well.

**Access.** From road 46, take road 4600-500 where you see the sign for "Lava Lake Resort." After 0.6 miles, this road forks, with the left fork going to Lava Lake and the right fork to Little Lava Lake. There is a message board at this fork. The right fork (road 4600-520) is two-lane gravel and ends at Little Lava Lake in less than a mile.

There is a trail from Little Lava Lake to Lava Lake. It starts in the

An abundance of shoreside reeds makes Little Lava Lake look like it might be productive water. Unfortunately, it is not.

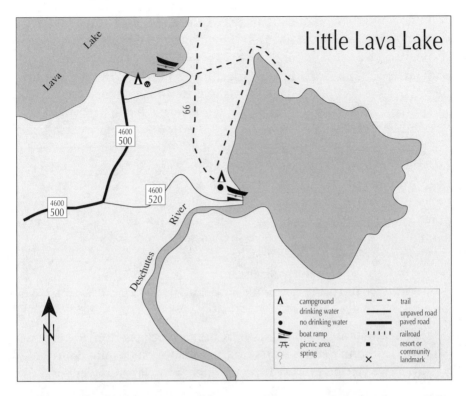

Little Lava Lake

| | | | |
|---|---|---|---|
| ∧ | campground | - - - | trail |
| ⊙ | drinking water | —— | unpaved road |
| • | no drinking water | ▬▬ | paved road |
| ⛵ | boat ramp | ı ı ı ı ı | railroad |
| 🏕 | picnic area | ■ | resort or |
| ⛲ | spring | | community |
| | | ✕ | landmark |

campground of Little Lava.

A trail goes part way around the north end of Little Lava and provides access to that shore. After a while, however, it peters out, and subsequent paths are used more by deer than by anglers.

**Camping and Recreation Sites.** Little Lava Lake Campground is a primitive campground with few amenities other than outhouses and a gravel boat launch. Most sites are by the lake near the boat launch. A few additional sites on the Deschutes River are off a spur road (turn-around is limited if you have a large rig), but the Forest Service has plans to close this area to camping.

Camp sites with tables and fire pits are scattered throughout, but there are no designated sites. There is no water, no trash dumpsters, and no fee.

**How to Fish Little Lava Lake.** At first glance, Little Lava looks like a productive lake, with a heavy growth of reeds around most of the shore. Unfortunately, underwater weed growth is minimal, and there is little of the aquatic life necessary for consistently good fishing.

A large population of chub live here. Besides these, many whitefish come into the lake from the Deschutes River. The result is too much competition for too little food, which is why fishing can be poor. If you come here in early season, you might find some fish. But if there has been a hard winter, and if the lake has not been stocked for a while, you can find it as dead as old horseshoes. It is possible that hungry trout migrate down the river and end up in Crane Prairie.

For the most part, this is a shallow lake. The northern third is deepest, with maximum depths along the rocky shore (contrary to bathymetric charts that have been issued for this lake). Here the bank is steep and rocky, and underwater springs in the northwest corner lower the temperature. This is a good place to start fishing in hot weather. The rest of the time, trout could be anywhere in the lake. Or nowhere.

Because there is a trail that gives access to the northwest part of the lake, it is a good place for bank-fishing.

Midges are the primary aquatic food, and fly-fishers can be effective here during an evening hatch.

**Fishing Regulations.** Open from the fourth Saturday in April to October 31. Up to five trout per day may be kept, with a six-inch minimum. Only one trout over 20 inches may be kept. There is no limit on whitefish.

**Boating Regulations.** 10 mph maximum speed.

## North Twin Lake

Size: 130 acres    Elevation: 4,330 feet

North Twin Lake is a small, deceptively deep lake with 9-11 inch stocked rainbow trout. There is a primitive campground at the lake, but more extensive facilities—including a resort—are nearby at South Twin Lake.

The lake basin is a maar, a volcanic creation that results from the explosive contact of hot magma with groundwater. This formed a crater a half mile across and over 50 feet deep. While fishing the lake, you can contemplate the equivalent tons of TNT needed to make a hole this size.

This is a family-oriented lake like South Twin, but not as busy. The lake shore is accessible, and most of the fishing is along the margins.

**Access.** Road 4260-050, a two-lane gravel road, heads south off road 4260 and ends a quarter mile later at the lake and campground. There is a sign for "North Twin Lake" on road 4260. No other roads are open to

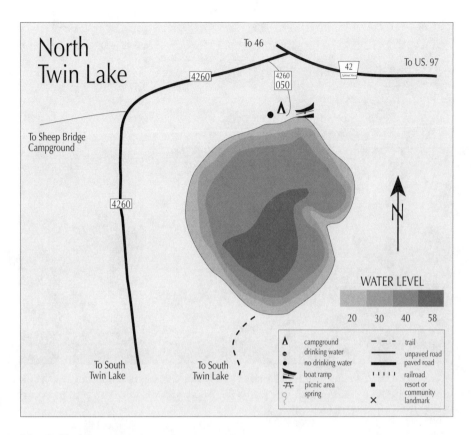

North Twin.

It is possible to walk around the entire shoreline, a distance of about a mile and a half. Many dead snags still stand near the shore, but many more have fallen down. This makes walking difficult in some areas, especially in early season when the water is highest.

There is a short trail between North Twin and South Twin. It starts at the south end of the lake, just opposite the boat ramp, and ends in the South Twin campground.

**Campgrounds and Recreation Sites.** North Twin Lake Campground is a busy, minimal service campground. There are a dirt boat launch, pit toilets, and a few tables, some of which have fire pits nearby. Dust can be a problem since none of the roads are paved. There are no drinking water, trash pickup, or designated sites. And no fee.

**How to Fish North Twin Lake.** The lake drops off quickly from shore, and it can easily be 25 feet deep only 100 feet from the bank. Weed

A jumble of snags rims much of North Twin Lake. A good fishing tactic is to walk around the lake casting a spinner, then halfway around take the trail to South Twin Lake and fish there, too.

growth and downed timber occur sporadically around the lake. These features, combined with the accessibility of the shoreline, make North Twin a good lake to fish from shore.

The rainbow here are all stockers, and reach about 11 inches by the end of the season. Larger fish are sometimes caught, but most of your catch will look like they came out of the same mold.

These trout are not sophisticated, but they aren't bloody stupid, either, especially those that last until the end of the season. Therefore, you have to do a few things right to catch them.

Most fishing here is with Power Bait, nightcrawlers, spinners, or flies. Almost all fish are within 150 feet of shore, except when the water is particularly warm and they seek deep water, or during a midge hatch when a few trout will cruise the pelagic surface in search of midge pupae.

An enjoyable and effective strategy is to circle the entire shore on foot, stopping every 50 or 100 feet to make several casts with a spinner.

In fact, you could make a day of it by going half-way around North Twin, taking the trail to South Twin (stopping at the resort for a hamburger lunch), fishing around South Twin, then back to finish up North Twin. You get a nice walk, some good fishing, and a hot lunch. That's not a bad way to spend a summer day.

Fly-fishing at North Twin can be quite good. The primary hatches are midges, *Callibaetis*, and caddis. Dries and nymphs are both effective. Damselfly nymphs and small Woolly Buggers also produce fish.

Most people who bring a boat to North Twin shoot themselves in the foot. They use the boat to reach the middle of the lake, and fish where there are few fish. The best way to use a boat here is to position yourself 50 to 100 feet off shore and use bait off the bottom, or cast a spinner or fly to the bank. It is not unusual to see a hatch at North Twin where 90% of the rises are within 20 feet of shore.

**Fishing Regulations.** Open from the fourth Saturday in April to October 31. Up to five trout per day may be kept, with a six-inch minimum. Only one trout over 20 inches may be kept.

**Boating Regulations.** No motors allowed.

# Odell Lake

Size: 3,600 acres    Elevation: 4,790 feet

This large, deep lake is right at the crest of the Cascades and offers excellent fishing for kokanee and mackinaw, as well as rainbow trout. There are two resorts and five campgrounds, one of which can only be reached by boat. Odell is a scenic lake surrounded by tall fir trees. The Diamond Peak Wilderness Area stretches just south of the lake, and you can enjoy breath-taking views while catching trophy fish.

A major state roadway, Highway 58, runs between I-5 and US 97 and skirts the north shore of the lake, so access is excellent. Of the lakes covered in this book, Odell is the closest by car to the metropolitan areas of the Willamette Valley.

Odell Lake was created by a glacier that scoured a deep, steep-sided trough. Parts of the east end are over 280 feet deep, and more than 96% of the lake is over 10 feet deep.

More than 6,000 years ago, heavy ash fall from Mt. Mazama (which formed Crater Lake) blanketed the area. The result is highly permeable soil, so moisture easily runs downhill and into the lake. Over 30 creeks

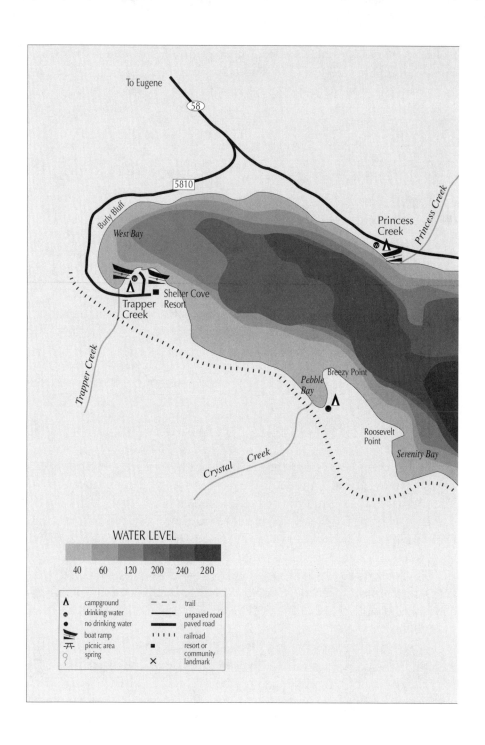

To Eugene

58

5810

Burly Bluff

West Bay

Princess
Creek

Princess Creek

Trapper
Creek

Shelter Cove
Resort

Trapper Creek

Pebble
Bay

Breezy Point

Roosevelt
Point

Serenity Bay

Crystal   Creek

## WATER LEVEL

40   60   120   200   240   280

| | | | |
|---|---|---|---|
| Λ | campground | – – – | trail |
| ⊚ | drinking water | ——— | unpaved road |
| ● | no drinking water | —— | paved road |
| ⟲ | boat ramp | ∎∎∎∎∎ | railroad |
| 禾 | picnic area | ■ | resort or |
| ⚲ | spring | | community |
| | | ✕ | landmark |

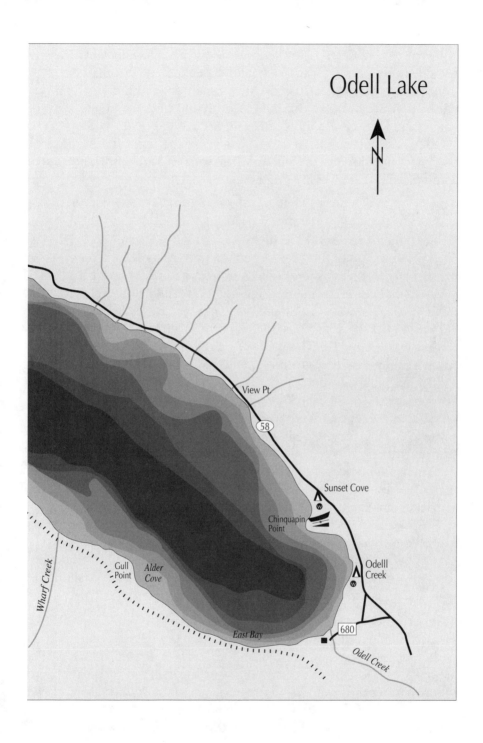

Odell Lake

N

View Pt.

58

Sunset Cove

Chinquapin
Point

Gull
Point

Alder
Cove

Odelll
Creek

East Bay

680

Wharf Creek

Odell Creek

and springs feed Odell. They keep the water at a near constant level and provide nutrients necessary for healthy aquatic life. The major inflow is from Trapper Creek, which is also the primary spawning water for kokanee. Odell Creek flows out the east end and becomes the source of water (and an occasional kokanee) for Davis Lake.

Because the lake is large and has no speed limit, it is sometimes used by water-skiers in the summer. The west end and north shore have a number of vacation homes on Forest Service leases.

**Access.** Highway 58 rims most of the north shore, providing views of the lake and Diamond Peak. Two campgrounds—Princess Creek and Sunset Cove—are just off this highway.

The west side of the lake is reached from road 5810, a paved road that intersects Highway 58 about 27 miles east of Oakridge and 32 miles west of Chemault. Turn at the sign for "W. Odell Lake/Campground." Road 5810 goes two twisting miles to Trapper Creek Campground and Shelter Cove Resort. Just past the resort turn-off, road 5810 ends at the resort's boat ramp. This last piece of road is gravel and passes near the resort's campground, so go slowly to avoid raising dust.

To reach the east end of the lake, turn off Highway 58 where there is a sign for "E. Odell Lake/Campground/Resort-Marina." This puts you on road 5800-680, which is paved. A half mile down this paved road you come to a bridge over Odell Creek. Odell Creek Campground is on one side and the resort is on the other.

There are no desirable ways to reach the shores of Odell Lake other than these access points. There are pull-outs on Highway 58, but they are better suited to picnicking and admiring the view than to fishing access. Spur roads off Highway 58 and road 5810 lead to summer homes on Forest Service leases. These should be treated as private property.

Highway 58 is heavily used by trucks, so give plenty of warning before turning off to the lake. When a fully-loaded log truck is sitting on your tail, it's a bad idea to suddenly stand on your brake pedal.

**Campgrounds, Recreation Sites, and Services.** Not only is Odell Lake blessed with excellent fishing, but it has two fine resorts—one at each end of the lake—and beautiful campgrounds set among tall firs. There are only two problems with camping here: the highway to the north and the railroad to the south. If you're not used to the sound of night time traffic, the nocturnal noises can get on your nerves.

*Shelter Cove Resort.* Shelter Cove Resort is at the west end of Lake on road 5810. As the name implies, the resort is sheltered from t prevailing westerly winds that sweep down the lake. The resort's campground is worth considering because it is sheltered from the wind and is larger than the popular Forest Service campground at Trapper Creek. The phone number for the resort is 503-433-2548; address mail to Shelter Cover Resort/West Odell Lake Road, Hwy 58/Cascade Summit, OR 97425.

Resort facilities include:

> Eight cabins, all with kitchen, some with wood stove; from $55 per night
>
> Campground from $8 per night; 69 sites in a forested setting
>
> Dump station (free to guests)
>
> Store with snack counter, sundries, limited groceries, and tackle (no flies); summer hours are M-Th 5-8, F 5-11, Sa 5-10, Su 5-6; winter hours are M-Th 6-7, F 6-10, Sa 6-9, Su 6-6
>
> Boat and motor rental
>
> Concrete boat ramp with dock (free for guests, $2 for others)
>
> Moorage
>
> Fishing tackle rental
>
> Fishing guide service

Shelter Cove Resort rents modern log cabins.

Gas and propane

Pay phone

*Odell Lake Lodge.* This resort serves the east end of the lake. You can relax in the rustic, log-walled comfort of the living room, enjoying the warmth and crackle of a fire in the stone fireplace, or sip a cooling beverage on the wooden deck. The phone number is 503-433-2540; send mail to PO Box 72, Crescent Lake, OR 97425.

Resort services include:

> Twelve cabins, all with kitchen and wood stove from $55 per night, plus 7 rooms in the lodge from $38 per night
>
> Restaurant; hours are M-Tu 5:30 PM-8, W-Su 8 AM-9 PM; closed M-Tu in winter
>
> Limited tackle, flies, and supplies
>
> Play area for children
>
> Boat and motor rental
>
> Concrete boat ramp (free for guests, $4 fee for others)
>
> Fish cleaning station
>
> Moorage
>
> Fishing tackle rental
>
> Fishing guide service
>
> Mountain bike rental

Odell Lake Lodge has a living room where you can curl up with a good book.

Gas and propane

Pay phone

*Trapper Creek Campground.* This is a popular campground, sheltered from the strong west wind. There are 32 designated sites, some of which are on the lake shore. A message board is at the entry. The gravel boat launch is in the middle of the campground, with trailer parking above it and on the other side of the boat ramp loop. Boaters often pull their craft onto a nearby beach and tie them to trees overnight.

*Pebble Bay Camp.* This boat-in camp site is at the head of Pebble Bay. A pit toilet and one picnic table with a fire pit are provided. Drinking water is not available, and there is no fee. The end of Pebble Bay is quite shallow, so be careful when beaching your boat.

*Princess Creek Campground.* Forty-five sites are spread among old-growth fir trees in this campground, and there is a fine view of Diamond Peak across the lake. Like some other Odell Lake campgrounds, you have a lullaby of passing Peterbilts through the night.

There is a message board at the entry. The boat ramp has a dock, and a small picnic area with two tables and one fire pit is nearby.

*Sunset Cove Campground.* The cove is open to the sunset, but also to the west wind. An "L" shaped dock at the boat ramp mitigates the wave action for those launching and landing boats.

This campground is similar to Princess Creek, with the same advantages and disadvantages. There are 26 designated sites on two loops. A well-shaded picnic area offers a good view of the lake and Diamond Peak. The picnic area has tables, water, and fire pits. Pit toilets are nearby.

*Odell Creek Campground.* The traffic noise from Highway 58 is lessened here, and you can concentrate on the rustle of fir needles as the wind passes through them. Actually, you will hear a lot of wind at this end of the lake, because it can whoosh down five miles of open water until it hits this shore. Make sure everything is tied down.

The usual Forest Service amenities, including drinking water, are provided to 22 designated sites, about half of which are on the lake shore. If you get tired of camp cooking, stroll over to Odell Lake Lodge; it has a restaurant. There is no boat ramp at the campground, but you can use the one at the lodge for a fee.

**How to Fish Odell Lake.** The major action here is kokanee, followed by mackinaw. The lake also contains rainbow trout, and fishing for them can be good for anglers who know where to look. All the fish populations are self-sustaining, if not indigenous.

The typical Odell kokanee is between 9 and 13 inches. This is a productive lake for kokanee, as is indicated by the possession limits. Fishing is concentrated in the west end of the lake, generally between Princess Creek and Trapper Creek. Check with the resorts to get an idea of how deep most of the fish are.

The kokanee here don't all hover at the same depth, and often stratify into several tiers. Fish at one level may not be receptive to your lure, but you might limit-out at a different level. Also, conditions can change and fish at a shallower depth may suddenly turn on. See Chapter 7 for more details about dealing with this phenomenon.

The kokanee techniques described in Chapter 7 work well here. Both trolling and jigging are productive, but jigging can be difficult (if not impossible) when the wind comes up. The lake is calm most mornings, but by afternoon it can turn to whitecaps.

By September, the mature kokanee begin their spawning migration, and you can start picking up dark fish after Labor Day. Let them go; they're not good eating at that point in their life, and a fish that is allowed to spawn will provide future dividends. Most spawning fish move toward Trapper Creek; the regulations prohibit fishing within 200 feet of Trapper Creek after August 31.

Kokanee are the primary forage fish for the lake's mackinaw, and the large, healthy kokanee population means large, healthy mackinaw. The state record mackinaw came from Odell, a fish that weighed over forty pounds. No doubt there are others of equal or larger size waiting for your lure, but the typical Odell mackinaw is between 10 and 20 pounds.

In 1991, more than 1,000 mackinaw over 15 pounds were landed at Odell Lake, but that kind of catch has not been seen since. Were all the dumb fish caught in 1991, leaving only the smart, slow-growing ones? Whatever, it is clear that Odell is a very productive mackinaw lake.

The mackinaw techniques described in Chapter 7 are suited to Odell Lake. Receptive macks fall into two categories: those which are suspended below the kokanee and prey on them, and those that sit on the bottom in deep water. In the first case, find the kokanee and you have found the mackinaw. This suggests a strategy of fishing kokanee in the early morning, then switching to mackinaw around 10 AM, trolling in the same places but perhaps 15 feet deeper.

The second case of bottom-lying mackinaw requires slightly different tactics. Good places to look for these fish are off Burley Bluff and along the north shore between Princess Creek and Chinquapin Point.

Odell Lake spreads across five square miles at the crest of the Cascades. The lake boasts trophy mackinaw and kokanee, as well as rainbow trout.

These fish are usually 100 to 150 feet deep.

In all cases, a lure that is kokanee-like is preferred. This means dark on top and light below. Jigging can also be productive, but should not be abused (see Chapter 7).

Odell Lake also has bull trout (formerly called Dolly Varden). Bull trout populations have declined significantly, and the regulations call for their release. Bull trout look a bit like mackinaw, but they have a more olive color instead of the mackinaw's gray tint. Also, mackinaw have a forked tail, where a bull trout's tail is more square.

Rainbow trout are an overlooked game fish in Odell Lake, with most people concentrating on kokanee and mackinaw. But good fishing for

Another Odell Lake kokanee is brought to the boat.

15-22 inch trout can be found if you know where to look. Because Odell has so little shoal area and high winds, there is little aquatic vegetation. The result is limited trout habitat. However, "limited" does not mean non-existent. Ply the south shore and some of the protected coves with midge pupae, woolly buggers, and damsel nymphs.

**Fishing Regulations.** Open from the fourth Saturday in April to October 31. Up to five trout per day may be kept, with a six-inch minimum. Only one trout over 20 inches may be kept. There is no limit on whitefish. Up to 20 kokanee per day may be kept, but no more than five may be longer than 12 inches; the kokanee limit is in addition to the trout limit. Bull trout (Dolly Varden) must be released unharmed. Closed to angling within 200 feet of Trapper Creek from September 1 to October 31.

**Boating Regulations.** There are no special boating regulations.

## Paulina Lake

Size: 1,520 acres    Elevation: 6,350 feet

Early in the 1993 fishing season, a brown trout of over 27 pounds was taken from Paulina Lake. This was a new Oregon state record, and the largest brown trout in five western states. The state record kokanee is also from Paulina. And there are bigger browns and bigger kokanee out there. Rainbow trout are also available to anglers, and fish over ten pounds have been caught.

Paulina Lake and its near neighbor East Lake were once a single body of water occupying Newberry Crater. This caldera was formed by a volcano that blew out the insides of the mountain and left a basin that filled with water, much as Mt. Mazama's eruptions resulted in Crater Lake. Later volcanic activity raised a barrier in the middle of Newberry Crater, dividing the large lake in two. The last volcanic activity was 2,000 years ago, but geothermal springs continue to feed the lake.

This is a high, clear lake with a turquoise hue. The sides are steep, and there is very little shoal area—the average depth is over 160 feet, and less than 3% of the lake is under 10 feet deep. Despite this, it is quite productive, as can be seen from its record fish. One reason for this productivity is the chemicals that are added by the hot springs.

There is some seepage from East Lake to Paulina Lake, but the water level in Paulina is amazingly constant, especially considering there are no inlet streams. Paulina Creek is the only outlet; it flows to the Little Deschutes River.

Humans have visited the area for 10,000 years, but it was barren of

Guy Carl holds the state record brown trout he caught in Paulina Lake in 1993. His trophy tipped the scales at over 27 pounds. There are bigger browns in the lake. (Ross Martin photo)

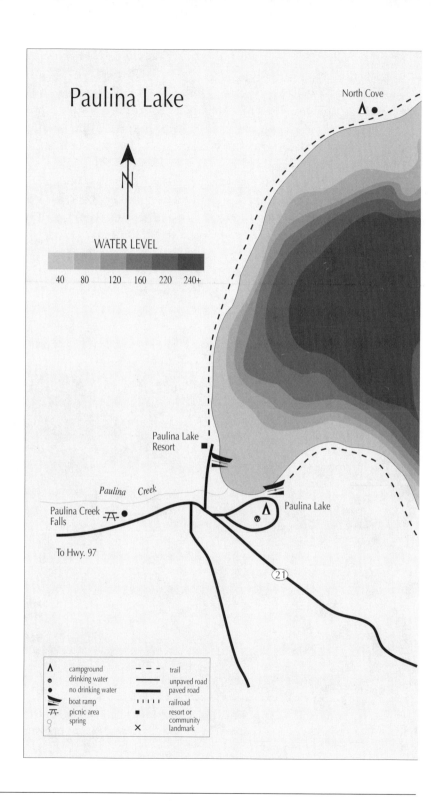

Paulina Lake

N

WATER LEVEL

40  80  120  160  220  240+

North Cove

Paulina Lake
Resort

Paulina   Creek

Paulina Creek
Falls

Paulina Lake

To Hwy. 97

21

| ⋀ | campground | – – – | trail |
| ☻ | drinking water | | unpaved road |
| • | no drinking water | | paved road |
| | boat ramp | ׀ ׀ ׀ ׀ ׀ | railroad |
| ⅋ | picnic area | ■ | resort or |
| ႞ | spring | | community |
| | | × | landmark |

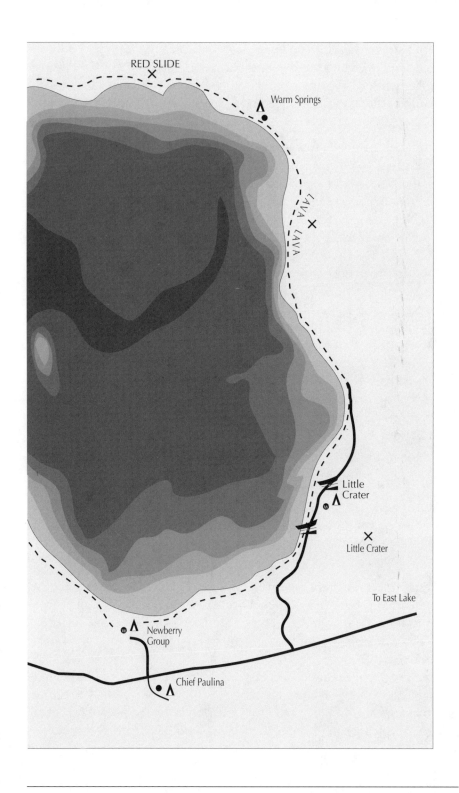

RED SLIDE

Warm Springs

LAVA LAVA

Little Crater

Little Crater

To East Lake

Newberry Group

Chief Paulina

fish until stocked with trout in the late 19th century. Sportsman have been coming ever since, and the old log resort was built in 1929 to serve them. There are also some summer homes on Forest Service leases.

Paulina Lake is easily reached on a paved road. Because it is so high, the fishing season opens later here than for other lakes in the region.

**Access.** Road 21 heads east from US 97, 22 miles south of Bend and six miles north of La Pine. A sign on US 97 directs you to East and Paulina Lakes; the turn-off to Paulina Lake Resort is 13 miles from US 97. Those who remember road 21's chuck-holed past will be glad to know that a major re-surfacing project is complete in 1994.

Paulina and East Lakes open somewhat later than the other lakes, and snow can block the road even after the opening of the fishing season.

The first road access point is Paulina Lake Resort, which is a short distance from road 21. The road to the resort closes about 9 PM and opens again at 6 or 7 AM; if you require access at other times, make arrangements with the resort.

Paulina Lake Campground is off road 21 just past the turn-off to the lodge, but on a separate spur that doesn't close at night.

Other than the Newberry Group Camp, there is no road access to the lake shore between Paulina Lake Campground and Little Crater Campground because road 21 is either too far from the lake or there are summer homes on Forest Service leases.

A couple of miles past Paulina Lake Campground there is a turn-off to Little Crater Campground (a sign marks the turn-off).

A trail (foot traffic only; no bikes) goes around the entire lake. The trail may be picked up at the resort, Paulina Lake Campground, or Little Crater Campground. It is 4.5 miles around the north shore from the re-sort to Little Crater Campground; another 2.5 miles completes the loop along the south shore.

**Campgrounds, Recreation Sites, and Services.** Fees for the Forest Service campgrounds are paid at a booth on road 21 several miles be-fore the lake. There are other campgrounds on road 21 as you come up to Paulina Lake, but they are not described here because they are too far from the fishing.

Paulina and East Lakes are high and exposed. It can be cold and windy here, so be prepared for all types of weather. Also, the entire Paulina Peak region has a healthy bear population. Follow the "bear country" guidelines in Chapter 1, and you should have no problems.

The log resort at Paulina Lake was built in 1929.

*Paulina Lake Resort.* The handsome log structures of the cabins, restaurant, and store hearken back to an earlier era of fishing, a time of bamboo fly rods with silk lines and gut leaders. Today you can enjoy the ambiance of a rustic past, then go out and catch lunker trout and kokanee on modern tackle. The restaurant closes at the end of September, but the cabins are available until the end of the fishing season. The resort can be reached at 503-536-2240; mail can be sent to PO Box 7, La Pine, OR 97739. Services include:

> Twelve cabins from $60 per night
> Restaurant open from 11:30 AM to 7:30 PM, closed Monday and Tuesday
> Store with sundries, limited groceries, tackle, and Teeny nymph flies
> Boat and motor rentals
> Boat ramp (free for guests, $5 for others)
> Moorage on limited basis; reservations required
> Gas
> Pay phones

*Paulina Creek Falls Picnic Area.* This pleasant day-use area is not on the lake, but is slightly downstream from it on the outlet creek. The turn-off is signed on road 21, shortly before the resort. A trail leads to

Paulina Falls. There are pit toilets, tables, and barbecues, but no drinking water.

*Paulina Lake Campground.* This popular campground has 69 designated sites tightly packed around small trees. Privacy is hard to obtain, which is why this campground is more popular with those owning RVs than with those who stay in tents. Most of the camp sites are a short distance from the lake.

By Forest Service standards, this is a posh campground with genuine flush toilets, running cold water, and electric lights in the rest rooms.

There are two boat ramps—a gravel one near the entry and a paved one in the middle of the campground. The latter ramp is better suited to large boats and has a dock and nearby fish cleaning station. Boats may be beached near either ramp.

A day-use area is located near the gravel boat ramp. It has tables and barbecues; rest rooms and drinking water are nearby.

*Chief Paulina Horse Camp.* This campground is not on the lake, but is on the south side of road 21 opposite the Newberry Group Camp. It is a horse camp with 14 designated sites. Four sites have four corrals, and the rest have two. Each corral has a chain gate. Stock water is provided, but drinking water is not. Reservations are required; call the Fort Rock Ranger District at 503-388-5674.

It is not unusual for black bears to rummage through the trash dumpsters at night, so make sure your stock is secure.

*Newberry Group Camp.* This campground is down a short paved road about one mile east of Paulina Lake Campground. Reservations are required; call the Fort Rock Ranger District at 503-388-5674. There are three group sites, each with a campfire circle and several tables placed close together for conviviality. There is no boat ramp here, but there are ramps nearby at Paulina Lake and Little Crater campgrounds.

*Little Crater Campground.* This large popular campground is on the east shore of the lake. See the access section for directions. There are 49 designated camp sites strung along a half mile of paved road. About half the sites are on the water.

A gravel boat ramp is a quarter mile from the junction with road 21, but there is a paved ramp with a dock farther on in the middle of the campground. Many boat owners beach their craft overnight on a sandy shore about two-thirds of the way through the campground. After beaching, tie the boat to a nearby tree.

Paulina Lake has two lakeshore camps which can only be reached by boat or by foot.

A day-use area is located near the gravel boat ramp at the entry. Tables and barbecues are provided, but you have to go into the campground for drinking water or toilets.

*Warm Springs Camp.* This is a rustic camp site that can only be reached by boat or by foot. It is spread out along a low shoreline east of the Red Slide. The western part has a sandy beach. There is a table here, but no fire pit or toilet. However, it does have one great amenity: a sandy bathtub with hot water. Feel around with your hand for the hot water (106 degrees!). The spring is right in the gravel, and you may need to make a shallow depression to collect the hot water, or it may already be done for you.

Farther east of this area (as you head to the lava flow) there are more tables and fire pits, and two pit toilets.

*North Cove Camp.* This is another rustic site for individualistic campers seeking solitude. It is set in big trees on the north shore of the lake and can be reached only by foot or by boat. The only facilities are a single pit toilet and a table with a fire pit.

**How to Fish Paulina Lake.** Paulina Lake is managed by ODFW for trophy brown trout and trophy kokanee. Rainbow trout fingerlings are also planted, but while a few holdovers grow to large size, most of the catch is under 12 inches. Because there are no inlet streams, there is no natural reproduction of any of these species, and all game fish are stocked. The lake also contains blue and tui chub, which provide forage for predatory fish.

Between the resort and Paulina Lake Campground there is a large shoal area. Most of it is under five feet deep with a mud bottom and few weeds. Game fish are not usually found in this water, although an occasional lunker brown wanders in looking for a MacMinnow burger.

If you are after kokanee, you must stay in the deep water portions of the lake. To do this, locate the point of land east of Paulina Lake Campground. Next, locate the last cabin in the resort (it has a red metal roof). A half mile north of this cabin there is a wooden nesting box nailed to a tree on the shoreline. Draw an imaginary line between the nesting box and the point, then stay east of that line and about 200 feet off either shore.

Beyond that imaginary line, kokanee can be almost anywhere in the rest of the lake, so check at the resort store to find out where people have been catching them most recently. The store puts up a chalk board that says what depth the kokanee are at. The kokanee techniques described in Chapter 7 work well in Paulina Lake. Fishing is best early in the morning and in the evening.

After Labor Day, the mature kokanee turn dark as spawning time nears. They will migrate toward Paulina Creek, but because they cannot get to running water, they cast their eggs in the lake. These dark fish are not good eating and should be released. ODFW gathers them and uses the eggs to raise kokanee for stocking here and in other lakes throughout the Northwest.

Successful fishing for brown and rainbow trout in this lake begins with an understanding of where to find the shoal areas. The rainbows inhabit the shoals because they have weed beds that produce the aquatic insects that the trout feed on. Small kokanee and chub also come into these areas for the same reasons. Large browns come into them to feed on the chub, kokanee, small trout, and crayfish.

The shoal areas where you are likely to find fish are:

*Off Newberry Group Camp,* there is a small, weedy area

*In front of the summer homes* between Newberry Group Camp and Little Crater Campground

*Between the two boat ramps* of Little Crater Campground

*Beginning at the north end* of the rocky area north of Little Crater

Campground and continuing around the lake past the Warm Springs and North Cove Camps about a half mile toward the resort

*In front of the resort cabins*

All these areas are suitable for bait-fishing, casting spinners, or fly-fishing, as well as trolling for large brown trout. The west shore near the resort cabins is a good evening fishing spot because the trees shade the water early.

Bait-fishing from the bottom up with Power Bait (see Chapter 7) is a commonly used method of catching rainbows and an occasional brown trout. Four-pound test line with a two-pound leader is preferred because of the clear water.

When fly-fishing for rainbows, use brown or black leeches, damselfly nymphs, or woolly buggers. I haven't seen very much *Callibaetis* activity here, but you should be prepared for it anyway. The lake has a large crayfish population, so you might want to carry a few patterns, or use a brown woolly bugger in rocky areas (see Chapter 6 about fishing crayfish patterns).

Look for midge hatches in the early morning and at dusk. These hatches are often away from the shoal areas in somewhat deeper water. Fish a pupa just subsurface, or try a Griffiths Gnat fished dry. In all cases, use long leaders (nothing less than nine feet) and thin tippets (4X is big, 5X is better) because the water is so clear.

If you are after trophy brown trout, keep in mind that all the dumb brown trout in the world were caught before the reign of Charlemagne. What we have today are smart, wary fish—shrewd and cautious through natural selection.

Brown trout are very security conscious. They are lovers of overhead cover, and feel safer when they have it, or at least have it nearby. Without the sense of security that comes from overhead cover, they are unlikely to pursue any kind of edible-looking objects, including your lure.

To a brown trout in a lake, "cover" can take many different forms, including darkness or low light, beds of floating weeds, boulder fields with nooks and crannies to hide in, downed timber or root wads, deep water, or wave action.

Thus, when a brown trout comes into a shoal area to feed on minnows, it prefers to do so under the cover of darkness, with the cover of deep water (or a boulder field, etc.) close at hand. Mr. and Ms. Brown want to grab their food, then head back to safety. If anything threatening comes along, they slide off to cover. It doesn't take much to send them on their way: one sloppy cast, a "clunk" in an aluminum boat, the pressure wave from trolling or wading near them. One hint of trouble and they are gone.

This means that the prime time to fish for browns is early morning or late evening, when there is little (or no) light. Overcast weather can make for good brown trout fishing all day, but there is no substitute for being on the water at those prime dawn and dusk hours.

In Oregon, you can begin fishing one hour before official dawn, and must quit one hour after official sunset. Serious brown trout anglers push this to the edge. They are on the water ready to fish when the mist is rising from the lake and you need a flashlight to tie on your lure. And in the evening, when everyone else is sitting around the fire talking about the big fish they almost hooked, the serious brown trout anglers are on the water, quiet and cautious as their quarry.

Most of the trophy brown trout are taken by trolling minnow lures such as those made by Rapala. Size 9 lures with black back and silver sides, or black with gold sides (or perch) work well.

When trolling these plugs, stay close to shore, and keep some distance between your boat and your lure; most good anglers strip out at least 200 feet of line, and some strip out much more. Electric motors are a good tool for trollers because they are quiet and less likely to spook wary browns.

In Paulina Lake, most of the best water is less than 20 feet deep. The habits of brown trout mean that the prime areas to seek them in this lake are in shoals next to drop-offs and ledges. The more sudden the drop-off, the more likely you'll find brown trout.

Paulina Lake has several little coves with rocky underwater structure. Most are close to deep water. Remember that a cove has a lot of shore area in relation to the amount of water it embraces. For a brown trout, this means a large hunting ground with an exit close by and a boulder field to hide in if the exit is blocked. What more could a predator want?

These coves are worth exploring with a cast lure (Rapala makes some) or a fly. But remember: one sloppy cast and you lose. Trophy fish don't give second chances.

These browns can be caught on a fly. Because a fly can't be cast very far, you have to get close to the fish, and float tubes are a good way to do this since they are quiet and present a low profile. Casts have to be accurate and subtle. Smacking the water with your fly, or letting the fly, leader, and line land in a big pile on the water near a fish, are not going to get you any brown trout.

One fly-fishing approach is to use a big streamer fly on a sinking line. Fishing near the bottom in 15 or 20 feet of water in brown trout territory is a good strategy. A slow troll in a float tube with a stripping retrieve can be effective, and the depth separates you from the fish. Also, by trolling the fly you don't have to cast as much and risk a bad cast.

Another approach is to cast into shallow water with a sinking line and let your fly settle to the bottom. After patiently waiting for everything to quiet down, begin your retrieve. Retrieve so the fly stays deep and follows the contour of the bottom. Are you going to lose flies doing this? Yes, but how badly do you want to catch that brown trout?

Brown trout are opportunistic feeders, attacking almost anything that looks alive. Leech patterns are good for them, as are streamer flies that look like baitfish. Try Wool Head Sculpins, Matuka-style flies, and Zonkers. Woolly Buggers in brown or olive are another good choice. Don't be afraid to use a small fly, such as a size 10. Just because the trollers are out there with plugs nine inches long, don't feel obligated to throw a fly of equal size.

The conventional wisdom about brown trout is that they are caught on shallow-running plugs trolled fast. Look at Bob Jones's three brown

Trolling for kokanee at Paulina Lake.

trout in the section on Wickiup Reservoir. They were caught on flies re-trieved slowly in deep water. So much for conventional wisdom. By the way, Bob used a type 4 full-sinking line. I fished the same place, using the same presentation and the same fly. The only difference was that I used a type 3 line and wasn't quite as deep as Bob. He caught the fish, and I took the pictures. Shortly after that I bought a type 4 line so I could fish deeper, and it's picked up some pretty nice browns. Being at the right depth really is critical.

The brown trout in Paulina Lake can be huge, and there are far more of them out there than most anglers suspect. However, they are tough to catch because they are so wary. Even if you are expert with fly, plug, spoon, or spinner, you are not going to get one every time you go out. Successful brown trout fishing calls for patience and dedication, and doing a lot of little things right. The experts are dedicated to their craft and understand their quarry. They rise when it's cold and dark and are on the water ready to fish at the first opportunity, and they are back out again at the end of the day. And they conserve the resource by returning their catch to the water so it can be pursued again.

**Fishing Regulations.** Open from Saturday prior to Memorial Day week-end to October 31. Up to five trout per day may be kept, with a six-inch minimum. Only one trout over 20 inches may be kept. (Note: for regu-lation purposes, kokanee are considered a trout).

**Boating Regulations.** 10 mph speed limit.

# South Twin Lake

Size: 120 acres    Elevation: 4,300

This is a friendly, civilized little lake stocked with rainbow trout. Services are excellent and include a full-service campground, resort, and nearby RV park. South Twin Lake is very popular with families, who come to camp, fish, swim, and relax in the sunshine.

At this lake, you are rarely far from the sound of children. Quite a few millennia ago, however, a different sort of sound was heard here: one heck of a bang. Hot magma pushed up through the earth and con-tacted ground water. This created vast quantities of super-pressurized steam which exploded and left a crater a half mile across. This geologic creation is called a "maar." The maar filled with water and made South Twin Lake. North Twin was formed by the same process.

There are no inlets or outlets to this lake. All the water is from seepage and snow melt.

A special feature of South Twin Lake is the absence of mosquitoes. The steep porous soil is not good habitat for them, and swallows and bats eat the few that emerge.

South Twin Lake was a favored fishing haunt of former president Herbert Hoover. He had a cabin on the shore, and fished both the lake and the nearby Deschutes River before Wickiup Dam was built. When Wickiup Reservoir filled in, the water level in South Twin rose a few feet, and Hoover's cabin had to be moved up the bank. Twin Lakes Resort rented it out until 1991 when a huge wind-toppled ponderosa pine destroyed it.

**Access.** A sign on 4260 directs you to the resort, which is very near the road. As you enter, the boat launch is straight ahead, the resort to your right, and the day-use area and campground to your left.

There is a mile-and-a-half shore-side walking trail around the lake. A rough bicycle trail is located farther up the bank.

A short trail leads to North Twin Lake. This trail begins in the campground near camp site 11 and is about a half mile long.

## Campgrounds, Recreation Sites, and Services.

*Twin Lakes Resort.* This is a complete resort, including a restaurant, cabins, RV park, and other tourist-oriented facilities. The staff is friendly and service-oriented. The resort is open until mid-October. Phone numbers are 503-385-2188 (April-October) or 503-593-6526 (November-March); address mail to PO Box 3550, Sunriver, OR 97707.

South Twin is a good place to take children fishing. It's a fun lake for grownups, too!

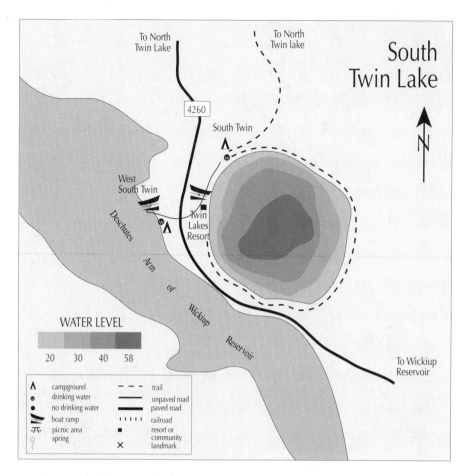

Resort facilities include:

> Seven individual log cabins and two lakeside studio four-plexes, all with kitchens; from $58 per night

> RV park with full hook-ups; located near the Deschutes channel of Wickiup Reservoir; $15 per night

> Restaurant (open summers from 6 AM to 9 PM; fall 8 AM to 8 PM)

> Convenience store with supplies, sundries, and tackle, including a few flies

> Rowboat, canoe, kayak, and paddleboat rentals

> Boat and motor rental for Wickiup Reservoir

> Fishing guide service

> Gasoline and propane

> Showers and laundromat

> Emergency phone

*South Twin Campground.* This is a pleasant, well-shaded, full-service campground on the lake shore. With a wealth of nearby activities that will amuse children as well as adults, it is very popular with families. If you get tired of over-roasted hot dogs with soot garnish, you can walk across the street to the resort's restaurant.

There is a day-use area between the boat launch and the camp sites. This area has tables, barbecues, and a building with running cold water, flush toilets, and changing rooms for swimmers.

The camping area has 21 designated sites with all the usual Forest Service amenities, including drinking water, pit toilets, some flush toilets, and garbage dumpsters. Tables and fire pits are provided at each camp site. There is a fee. The boat launch is between the day-use area and the resort.

**How to Fish South Twin Lake.** South Twin Lake is a rainbow trout fishery. It is stocked each year with both three to four inch fingerlings and 9-12 inch trout. Fishing can be excellent, with most of the catch between 10 and 14 inches. Every year a few fish over five pounds are taken.

Unlike its near neighbor North Twin, this lake has good submerged weed beds around much of its shore. These provide homes for damselflies, dragonflies, crayfish, *Callibaetis*, caddisflies, and midges. The lake is ringed with ponderosa pines. Over the years, a few of these have fallen into the lake and provided additional aquatic habitat (and places for anglers to get snagged).

This is a deep lake, despite its small size. The bottom drops off sharply all around the lake, although the east side is less abrupt. A common mistake on this lake is to fish too deep. The trout are seldom more than 30 feet from the surface, and most fishing should be within 300 feet of shore. Check the water depth by measuring how much anchor line you put out, and try to stay 15 to 30 feet deep.

Power Bait is the most common tactic on the lake (see Chapter 7 for how to use it), however flies, spinners, and small lures can work well, too.

Since so many of the fish are close to shore, bank fishing can be effective. The trail around the lake provides good access. One area that is not good for bank fishing is in front of the campground's day-use area.

These might be unsophisticated stocked trout, but you should not take them for granted. They are line shy, and you should stick to leaders of four pounds or less, and keep them two to four feet long. Fly-fishers should use a nine foot, or even 12 foot, leader tapered to 5X; keep the tippet relatively long if you cast well.

Fly-fishing can be excellent here. The lake is small enough that it can be easily covered from a float tube. The northwest shore is a good place to ply with damselfly nymphs, and the ever-productive size 14 Pheasant Tail nymph is another good option. Midge, leech, and caddis patterns are also good choices. There is a fairly reliable midge hatch around 11 AM most summer days, as well as evening hatches. Watch for caddis hatches (see Chapter 6). If one happens, offer an Elk Hair Caddis that matches the size of the hatching insects.

**Fishing Regulations.** Open from the fourth Saturday in April to October 31. Up to five trout per day may be kept, with a six-inch minimum. Only one trout over 20 inches may be kept.

**Boating Regulations.** No motors allowed.

# Sparks Lake

Size: 400 acres     Elevation: 5,400 feet

All lakes are dying. From the moment of their birth they are filling with silt from inlet streams, and vegetation is encroaching from the margins. Sparks Lake is a prime example of this process. The remnant of a bigger and deeper lake, it is now in the final stages before becoming a mead-ow. This isn't going to happen tomorrow, however, and while this fly-fishing-only lake goes through its dotage, it offers good early season angling for brook trout.

Sparks is a very shallow lake—nowhere more than 12 feet deep—with three inlet streams. While there is no outlet, water is lost by evapo-ration over the extensive surface area, and by seepage through the lava dam that created the lake. The water level can drop three feet or more by the end of the season, exposing much of the lake bed. The Forest Service has plugged some of the leaks in the lava dam, and this keeps the lake higher than it might be otherwise.

As you might expect, the drought years have been hard on Sparks Lake. At one time, the brook trout fishery was incredible, with fat three-pounders everywhere. The fish now are much smaller, but this is still an interesting and enjoyable lake.

The prime season for Sparks can be short. Heavy snow sometimes blocks access until late May, and warming water can turn the fishing off by July. Because of the short season, facilities here are primitive and minimal, but many of Sparks' visitors like it that way.

Sparks Lake is located near South Sister, Broken Top, and Mt. Bachelor, and the mountain views make it a scenic spot all season. In addition to anglers, the lake attracts canoeists, who don't mind the shallow water and spend many hours exploring the slender, lava-sided reaches and coves.

**Access.** Road 46 skirts the north shore of Sparks Lake, although at this end it looks more like a meadow than a lake. Road 4600-400, a two-lane gravel road, heads south from 46; there is a sign on 46. Near the beginning of this road, a rough unnumbered dirt road forks to the right; it ends at Soda Creek, still some distance from the lake. The main road goes 1.7 miles and ends at about the middle of the lake, where there is a picnic area with a concrete boat ramp.

At the northwest end of the lake, where Satan Creek comes in, there is an unmarked turn-off onto a rough single-lane dirt road. This is road 4600-426, although the number is hard to read on the sign post. There are primitive camp sites at the end of this road.

A trail heads southwest from the Sparks Lake trailhead near the beginning of road 400. This trail touches the southern corner of Sparks Lake two-and-a-half miles later. It continues to a bluff overlooking Hosmer Lake, where it splits, with one fork going northwest in a pretty trek along Quinn Creek as far as Quinn Meadow Horse Camp. The other

Broken Top is one of three mountains that ring Sparks Lake.

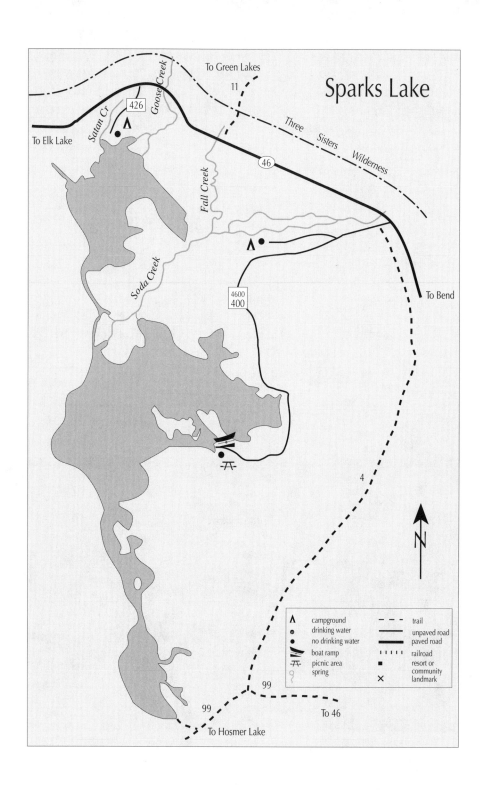

Sparks Lake

To Green Lakes

11

Goose Creek

426

Satan Cr

To Elk Lake

Fall Creek

Three Sisters Wilderness

46

Soda Creek

4600
400

To Bend

4

N

campground
drinking water
no drinking water
boat ramp
picnic area
spring

trail
unpaved road
paved road
railroad
resort or
community
landmark

99

99

To 46

To Hosmer Lake

fork proceeds due south three boring miles to Lava Lake.

At the boat ramp, there is another trail that heads off from a new (1993) trailhead and parking area. This is the Ray Atkeson interpretive trail, named for the well-known Oregon photographer. It has handicapped access, and was designed and built by a citizen-Forest Service partnership. The trail comes near the lake, but is not useful for fishing access.

**Camping and Recreation Sites.** All camping at Sparks Lake is primitive. None of the sites have drinking water or trash dumpsters, but then again they are free.

Some people camp at the northeast corner, at the end of the dirt road that joins road 400. This area is often used by RVs, but there is poor access to the lake here. There are a few tables, and a pit toilet is located back in the trees.

Several small tent sites that overlook the lake are scattered along road 400. At the end of this road there is a day-use area with one table, a concrete boat ramp, and a pit toilet. The toilet is hidden in the trees about 100 yards from the boat ramp. Cross your legs and keep looking; you'll find it eventually.

The end of road 4600-426 at the north corner of the lake has two camping spots. Both are set in big trees at the edge of the meadow bordering Satan Creek. You can launch a canoe in the creek and travel to the lake if the water is high enough. The only amenity at this camping area is a pit toilet. Bring bug sauce. Lots of it.

**How to Fish Sparks Lake.** The brook trout you find will be eight to thirteen inches long, with an occasional fish over 16 inches. Most are plump, having sufficient food for the number of fish that are present. ODFW stocks fish each year, but there is also substantial natural reproduction in the tributary creeks.

Prime time for Sparks Lake is early season, shortly after ice-out and when the roads are cleared. The water level is at its highest then, and fish can be scattered. The best advice for a brook trout lake is to fish the margins, but Sparks is all margins. The fish could be anywhere.

Later in the season, fish tend to congregate at the south end where the water is deepest. Getting to that part of the lake is hard work unless you have a canoe. The bottom in this part of the lake is uneven. Seek out the deeper water; it is a darker color.

The water tends to be clear in early season, so long leaders and fine

South Sister rises abruptly from the meadows around Sparks Lake.

tippets (5X maximum, 6X better) are the rule. Long leaders mean harder casting, and thin tippets require good quality rods and reels to keep feisty fish attached to you.

The primary hatches are caddis and midges. There are a few leeches, and the scud population can be phenomenal. ODFW says they have even found small toads in stomach samples!

Boating in Sparks Lake is difficult later in the season when the level has dropped. Float tubes are effective, but with so much surface area it is hard to cover the lake well in one. Canoes are good for getting around in the lake, but have their own set of problems for fly-fishers.

Approach the fish carefully; they will be spooky in shallow clear water. Cast gently. Enjoy the scenery and wildlife. Be patient. This is not an easy lake to fish.

**Fishing Regulations.** Open from fourth Saturday in April to October 31. Fly-angling only. Up to 10 trout per day may be kept, with a six-inch minimum. No more than five trout over 12 inches, and no more than two over 20 inches. You may not fish from a boat while its motor is operating.

**Boating Regulations.** 10 mph speed limit. See the restriction above about not fishing while the motor is operating.

# Todd Lake

Size: 45 acres    Elevation: 6,151 feet

Small, but popular, Todd Lake rests near the foot of Broken Top. It offers stocked brook trout in a pleasant setting. The lake is shaped like Florida, but is not nearly as warm. Be prepared for mosquitoes, though.

Todd Lake sits in a glacial valley, which is why it is so deep (over 50 feet). The north end has a sloping meadow with three small creeks that trickle into the lake. An outlet stream is at the south end.

A road goes most of the way to the lake, but you have to walk the last quarter mile. There are camp sites at the lake for those who pack everything in (including water) and take out all their trash. This is a heavy snow area, and it is not unusual for the road to be closed until late June or early July.

Todd Lake was originally called Lost Lake. There are so many Lost Lakes in Oregon (those pioneers spent a lot of time wondering where the heck they were) that the name was changed to honor John Y. Todd, who built the first commercial bridge over the Deschutes River at Sherars Falls.

**Access.** A gravel road, 4600-370, leads a half mile to the parking area. The road continues, but you park here and walk about a quarter mile up another road (behind the parking area) to reach the lake. This road is closed to motor vehicles, but on it you see just about everything else that has wheels, from bicycles to baby carriages to wheelbarrows. The old road ends at the south shore of the lake, where there is a camping and picnicking area.

A trail goes around the lake shore, but early in the season it can get a little soggy in the north-end meadow. A hike to the ridge-top above the north end of the lake will reward you with a gorgeous view of Todd Lake and Mt. Bachelor.

**Camping and Recreation Sites.** You may not camp at the parking area, but if you pack all your gear up the trail, you will find pleasant camping. There are a pit toilet and several tables at the south end of the lake; fire pits are in bad repair. There are no water or trash pick-up, and no fee.

This is a park-like area, somewhat open but with big trees around and a nice view of Broken Top rising over the north end of the lake. Those who make the effort to pack in their gear and drinking water will be rewarded.

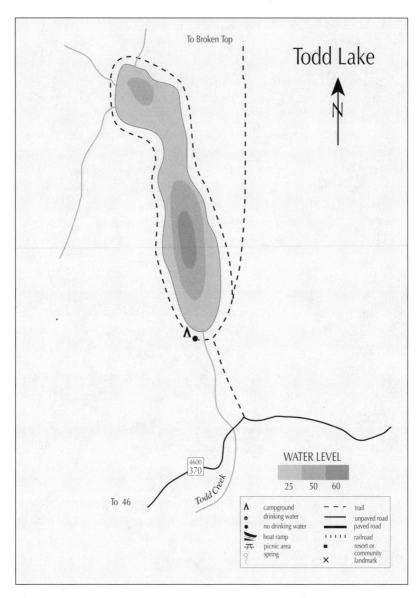

To Broken Top

Todd Lake

N

WATER LEVEL

25  50  60

4600
370

To 46

Todd Creek

Λ   campground
◉   drinking water
●   no drinking water
▬   boat ramp
⼨   picnic area
♀   spring

- - -   trail
———   unpaved road
▬▬▬  paved road
ı ı ı ı   railroad
■   resort or community
×   community landmark

**How to Fish Todd Lake.** Todd Lake is not a productive body of water; there is little weed growth, and the bottom is sandy. Still, it is an enjoyable place to fish for brook trout. The lake is stocked by helicopter, and there is also some natural reproduction. Most of the catch are nine or ten inchers, however an occasional 15 inch holdover is hooked.

While there are shoal areas, the lake is deceptively deep, and stratifies in summer with the thermocline around 20 feet. A common mistake

Broken Top peeks over the ridge above Todd Lake. This lake is cold and deceptively deep. A common mistake is to fish too deeply.

is to fish it too deeply. The water is clear, so use four-pound leaders or tippets of 5X or less. The trout are not of a size to put much strain on these thin lines.

The bottom drops away quickly from the shore, so bank-fishing is effective. Since there is a trail around the lake, a good strategy is to walk the shoreline casting spinners, bait, or flies. This gives you a nice walk while covering most of the available fish.

The primary fish food is midges. There are also some *Callibaetis* and leeches. Fly-fishers may want to pack in a float tube so they can reach mid-lake trout during the midge hatches.

Like most brook trout waters, Todd Lake is best early in the season. The road is often closed by snow well after the start of the season, and it is common for anglers to walk in after ice-out to catch the early season feeding frenzy. Those who make the effort will be rewarded with fish— and attacked by vast squadrons of voracious mosquitoes.

**Fishing Regulations.** Open from the fourth Saturday in April to October 31. Up to 10 trout per day may be kept, with a six-inch minimum. No more than five trout over 12 inches, and no more than two over 20 inches.

**Boating Regulations.** No motors allowed.

# Wickiup Reservoir

Size: 10,000 acres

Elevation: 4,350 feet

When it is full, Wickiup Reservoir is the largest body of water in the Deschutes National Forest, covering over 15 square miles. It is also one of the most productive reservoirs in the state, and offers kokanee, trophy brown trout, and landlocked coho salmon. Native Americans hunted and fished at this site as long as 10,000 years ago. Their temporary dwellings (wickiups) gave the area its name.

The Deschutes River is the main inflow, but water also enters

Bob Jones shows off three fly-caught brown trout he landed in Wickiup Reservoir. The top two fish were hooked in one evening, the bottom fish the next morning. All three trout were released.

from Davis Creek, Browns Creek, and Sheep Springs. The Deschutes is the only outflow. It was dammed in 1947 to create the reservoir.

Unlike neighboring Crane Prairie, Wickiup was logged before it was flooded. Although the timber was taken out, the root wads and stumps remained because people had no use for them. But the fish knew what to do with all that habitat and structure, and they flourished. Much of this woody material has now decayed, and ODFW is putting stumps and bundles of logs back into the lake for the benefit of the fish (and anglers).

Because Wickiup is a reservoir of irrigation water, it is drawn down throughout the summer, and a visitor that came in April and returned in October might question if it is the same body of water. Much of the lake is shallow, and by the end of the season vast territories of dry land are exposed. Access to Wickiup is quite good when it is at full pool, but campgrounds and roads that are suited to the early season can be miles from open water by fall.

There is a 10 mph speed limit in the Deschutes channel, but there is no speed limit on the rest of Wickiup, and the lake is used by water-skiers in the summer.

**Access.** Wickiup Reservoir has enough obscure dirt roads leading to its shores to sate the enthusiasm of the most indefatigable driver. Virtually no part of the lake is unreachable in high water, but when the reservoir is drawn down, access to fishable water is restricted to a few prime locations. These are West South Twin, Gull Point, and the face of the dam. As the reservoir level drops through the summer, many of the other access points mentioned here are far from open water.

At the north end of Wickiup Reservoir, road 4260 heads south from 42. From this road, there is access to Wickiup from road 4260-070 (a gravel road that turns to single-lane dirt) which goes to Sheep Bridge Campground, from West South Twin Campground, and from Gull Point Campground. After Gull Point, road 4260 turns to gravel and is back from the lake for two-and-a-half miles, then returns to it at the face of the dam.

Road 4260-950 (which feels like a continuation of 4260) crosses the top of the dam, providing fishing access the entire length; bank anglers often take advantage of this access early in the season. At the south end of Wickiup Dam, 4260-950 passes Wickiup Butte boat ramp and campground, and then joins road 44. Just before Wickiup Butte, right at the southeast end of the dam, there is a small turn-out where a float tube or

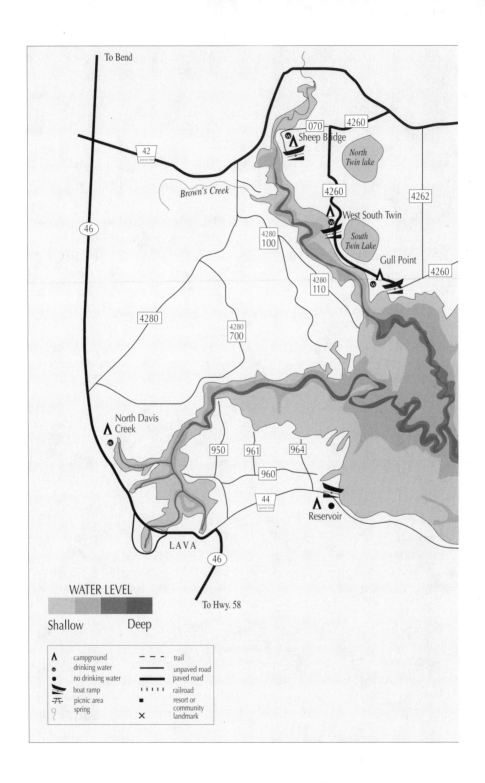

To Bend

42

Brown's Creek

46

070 Sheep Bridge

4260

North Twin lake

4260

West South Twin

4262

South Twin Lake

4280 100

Gull Point

4260

4280 110

4280

4280 700

North Davis Creek

950   961   964

960

44

Reservoir

LAVA

46

To Hwy. 58

WATER LEVEL

Shallow        Deep

Λ    campground
◉    drinking water
●    no drinking water
      boat ramp
🛝    picnic area
ᕊ    spring

- - -    trail
          unpaved road
          paved road
ı ı ı ı ı    railroad
■    resort or community
×    landmark

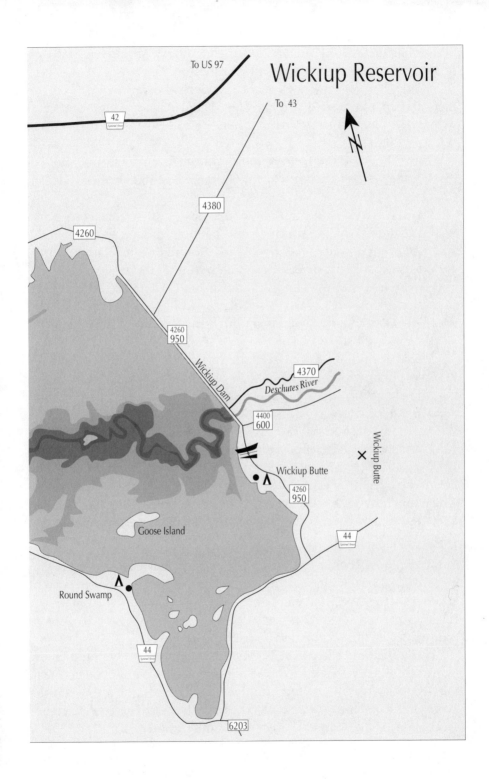

To US 97

Wickiup Reservoir

To 43

N

42

4380

4260

4260
950

Wickiup Dam

4370

Deschutes River

4400
600

Wickiup Butte

Wickiup Butte

X

4260
950

Goose Island

44

Round Swamp

44

6203

other small craft could be launched; trailered boats would have difficulty here because of large stumps on the shore.

Road 4380 is a straight two-lane gravel road that provides a convenient short cut from road 43 to the dam. There is a very rough boat ramp where 4380 joins 4260-950, but a better choice is to use the ramp at Wickiup Butte.

Two other roads come in near the dam: 4370, and 4400-600. Both of these come up the Deschutes River. They are described in more detail in Chapter 4.

Road 44 is a two-lane gravel road that passes the southeast corner of Wickiup, then skirts the southern shore before turning away from the lake and joining road 46. Reservoir and Round Swamp Campgrounds are off this road. East of Reservoir Campground, there is excellent access to the lake shore when the water is high. There are several turnouts along this stretch that provide good day-use spots, or even overnight camping; no facilities are provided, however. The junction of 44 and 46 is well-signed on 46.

There are numerous single-lane dirt roads that spur off 44 near Reservoir Campground. If you follow one these rough and dusty roads you will eventually reach the reservoir (if the water is high). These areas are often utilized by day users and self-contained campers.

Access to the west shore of Wickiup is from spur roads off road 4280, which goes between roads 42 and 46. None of these spur roads get very close to the water except 4280-110, which goes down the Deschutes Channel and is a spur off 4280-100, and road 4280-700, which touches the shore once along the Davis Creek Channel, and road 4280-050 which goes down Browns Creek (fishing in Browns Creek closes after August 31).

**Campgrounds, Recreation Sites, and Services.** In addition to the campgrounds and recreation sites described here, there are others nearby at South Twin and North Twin Lakes. The resort at South Twin serves Wickiup and rents boats with motors for use on the reservoir. The resort is described in the section on South Twin Lake.

Primitive camp sites for self-contained campers can be found along many of the roads that encircle Wickiup. They are mentioned above in the access section. Only the established campgrounds are described here. Gull Point and West South Twin are the only full-service campgrounds and have access to open water all season.

*Sheep Bridge Campground.* This campground is at the end of 4260-070, a half mile from 4260. There is a sign on 4260. This is a primitive campground whose limited facilities include a few tables with fire pits, drinking water, and pit toilets. There are no trash dumpsters. Sites are not designated, and no fee is charged. A rough gravel boat ramp is provided, but the water here is more river than lake.

*West South Twin.* While the name seems to imply a confusion in compass directions, it makes logical sense: this is the west part of the South Twin Lake Campground. The other half is across the road.

There is a sign on road 4260 directing you to this campground. There are 23 designated sites, and full services are provided. Sites 9-13 are tent-only sites. The concrete boat ramp is straight ahead as you enter the campground; ample parking is provided.

*Dump Station.* An RV sanitary dump station is located between the West South Twin and Gull Point campgrounds. There is a sign on road 4260.

*Gull Point Campground.* A sign on 4260 points to the entry to this large and popular campground. There is a message board at the entry. Camping is in 81 designated sites on two loops.

One concrete boat ramp is off the north loop (go right as you enter the campground) and has lots of parking. Another concrete ramp, known as the North Wickiup Boat Ramp, is on a road that is just past the south loop. This road intersects 4260, rather than the campground loop, so it can be reached when the campground is closed. Fish cleaning stations are located near both ramps. Day-use areas are also located near each boat ramp and have tables and barbecues; toilets and water are nearby.

*Wickiup Butte Campground.* This is a small camping area with no facilities other than a pit toilet and a few scattered tables. There is no fee. A paved boat ramp is a quarter mile north of the camping area on a spur off 4260. There is a pit toilet at the ramp.

*Round Swamp Campground.* This is an early season campground off road 44. It offers only a pit toilet. No water, no tables, no trash pickup, no boat ramp, and no fee. As the reservoir is drawn down, this area will be far from fishable water. Should anyone camp at a place that has "swamp" as part of its name?

*Reservoir Campground.* This is another early season campground. It is quite small, and the only camping facilities are pit toilets and a few tables, some of which have fire pits. There is a concrete boat ramp, but the water level doesn't have to drop much for it to be out of the water. There is no fee for camping here.

*North Davis Creek Campground.* At this time, the North Davis Campground is closed for rehabilitation.

**How to Fish Wickiup Reservoir.** Wickiup is most popular early in the season when it is full and the water skiers have yet to arrive. In addition to the kokanee, coho, and brown trout discussed below, Wickiup has a few rainbow trout and brook trout. Chub and whitefish are present and serve as forage for larger predatory fish.

Kokanee and landlocked coho salmon are the most popular fish. They scatter pretty well in the spring, but concentrations of kokanee can usually be found along the face of the dam and at the mouth of the Deschutes channel. Coho often gather near Goose Island. However, this situation can change fast as the water warms. As the season progresses, kokanee tend to move into the deeper water near the Deschutes channel. Later, they will migrate up the channel to spawn in the river.

The kokanee techniques discussed in Chapter 7 work well in Wickiup, and both trolling and jigging are popular. Coho can be taken on bait and lures.

Wickiup holds a few rainbows. The Davis Creek arm is a good place to seek them out.

Wickiup is also home to some monster brown trout. The state record used to be a Wickiup fish, but was replaced by one from Paulina.

In 1989 the brown trout fishery here was devastated by poachers who strung gill nets across Browns Creek and took out hundreds of big spawners. They said they thought the fish were carp. The poachers were caught, but many anglers felt that their sentence was too light and that the removal of certain body parts would have been appropriate.

The brown trout fishery has been recovering, though. In 1993, the largest fish weighed at Twin Lakes Resort was over 15 pounds, so there is hope for anglers.

The browns prey on kokanee, chub, whitefish, and anything else that looks like it might be alive. In spring, the prime places to find them are where the kokanee are also found, near Goose Island and the dam. Wickiup Butte and the mouth of the Deschutes channel between Gull Point and Eagle Point are also good areas for browns.

Refer to the section on Paulina Lake for a discussion of brown trout fishing in general. At Wickiup, there is little rocky structure such as found at Paulina, however there is lots of woody structure, and more is

Early morning launch at Gull Point.

being added. The Deschutes channel offers deep water and sudden drop-offs for the browns, and within the old river bed there is rocky structure. That is why most browns are caught in the channel or not too far from it.

As discussed in the section on Paulina Lake, browns have nocturnal feeding habits,so early morning and dusk are good times to seek them.

When it is full, Wickiup is a big reservoir. Therefore, when the wind blows it can get quite rough and become unsafe for small boats, especially in early season. However, the wind can be good news for well-prepared anglers with bigger craft. The wind and waves gather baitfish against windward shores and toss them around. The small fish cannot cope with the strong wave action, and the browns feed on them along the windward margins, using the rough water as overhead cover.

This is one of the reasons the area in front of the dam is a good spring fishing spot; the prevailing westerly winds push baitfish against it. Also, the strong spring outflows set up a current that pulls small fish to the dam, and the deep water of the Deschutes channel is nearby.

As fall approaches, the browns head up the Deschutes channel toward their spawning grounds in Browns Creek, Sheep Springs, and the Deschutes. The water north of the Gull Point boat ramp is closed after August 31.

A point of warning: it's easy to say that the fish are usually in or near

The face of Wickiup Dam in low water. The root wads provide habitat for bait-fish and brown trout in spring when the water is high. ODFW is dumping woody debris into the lake to provide more habitat.

the river channels, but finding those channels without an electronic fish finder is very difficult. There are few clues from the surface to tell you where the channels lie.

The lowly, under-respected whitefish thrives in Wickiup. Fish up to four pounds can be caught. It's quite possible that the next state record whitefish will come from Wickiup. (If you caught the state's biggest whitefish, would you tell anyone?) Whitefish readily take spinners and other lures, but they have small mouths. Therefore, small hooks are needed. The Davis Creek area is a good place to look for whitefish.

**Fishing Regulations.** Open from the fourth Saturday in April to October 31. Up to five trout per day may be kept, with a six-inch minimum. Only one trout over 20 inches may be kept. There is no limit on whitefish. Up to 25 kokanee and coho (in combination, not separately) may be kept each day, with no size restrictions and in addition to the trout limit.

*Browns Creek and the Deschutes River channel above Gull Point are closed after August 31.*

**Boating Regulations.** 10 mph in the Deschutes River channel (upstream from Gull Point) and Davis Creek arms.

# 3

# The High Lakes

For a few hardy anglers, the lure of the high mountain lakes is irresistible. These adventurers find the scenery more spectacular when they have to walk five miles to view it, and to them, the size of the trout is less important than elbow room and the satisfaction of exploring new territory.

Nearly all high lakes contain brook trout planted by ODFW. Brook trout are hardy fish that hold up well in the tough alpine environment, which is why they are the fish of choice here. However, the summer season is short at high elevations, and while the occasional five-pounder can be found, most fish do not grow to large size. Anglers visiting the high lakes should go with the expectation of catching solitude and scenery, but not trophy trout.

ODFW stocks all the lakes every other year, usually by helicopter. Some of the lakes with road access are stocked every year. Volunteers sometimes pack into the mountains to put trout *into* lakes, rather than take them out. While a few lakes hold cutthroat or rainbows, brookies are far and away the predominant fish in the high lakes.

Most of these lakes are small (under 40 acres), however a few, such as Mink Lake, are quite large. Very small ponds and creeks are often encountered when hiking in the area; they rarely contain fish. In addition, there are some fishy-looking lakes that are *not* stocked due to poor fish survival (e.g., Bingham Lakes).

Some of the hike-in lakes are close to the Cascade Lakes Highway (road 46), and can be reached on a good, nearly level trail. Others, such as the very popular Green Lakes, are longer hikes up steep trails that will test your lung and leg power.

There are several lake chains and lake basins within the Deschutes National Forest. These concentrations of still water make it possible to sample several lakes with little extra effort. For example, the Winopee Lake trail heads at Cultus Lake. After several miles, you reach Muskrat Lake. Then every mile or so up the trail a new lake is encountered. This offers many opportunities for anglers who like to explore. The Mink Lakes Basin is another area where, once you reach it, many lakes are concentrated in a small space.

**Getting to the High Lakes.** Most of the high lakes are reached by hiking in from a trailhead, although a few, such as Irish and Taylor, can be reached by dirt/gravel roads. Four-wheel drive is rarely needed for drive-in lakes (unless it rains), but a rugged vehicle with good ground clearance is essential.

Horses can be used to reach many of the lakes that have trails, but

Some people use horsepower to reach the high lakes.

when riders dismount and turn into anglers, they must take care to prevent their stock from abusing the landscape.

Mountain bikes are popular transport for some anglers, however they are not permitted in the Three Sisters Wilderness Area, within which many of the lakes lie.

If you fish the high lakes, sooner or later you are going to be a walker, and foot power rather than horse power is the way most people reach the lakes. Many lakes are within three miles of a trailhead, and so are suitable for a day trip by anglers who are in good shape.

Permits are required for anyone entering the Three Sisters Wilderness. They are available at trailheads and at the borders of the Wilderness Area.

Hike-in anglers should pay as much attention to their their feet as they do their fishing gear. Make sure you have good quality boots that are broken-in. Socks from synthetic material such as polypropylene are best because they wick moisture away from your feet. Cotton socks are the worst choice because they hold moisture next to the skin, which causes blisters to form.

Those going overnight should be experienced outdoor recreationists. If you haven't backpacked before, go with someone who has. A few of the lakes have rough wooden shelters, but most are in bad repair and backpackers should not count on them.

Even if you are not going in overnight, however, you should be prepared. *Always* carry a good topographical map (one with contour lines). Also, be prepared for sudden changes in the weather.

For the last 35 years I have been a zealous believer in the Ten Essentials:

    Map
    Compass
    Raingear and extra clothes in case of bad weather
    First aid kit
    Knife

Matches in waterproof case

Fire starter, such as a candle or chemical starter

Emergency food

Flashlight

Sunscreen

These items can be fitted into a small space and should go with you every time you trek into the woods. I have a small fanny pack with most of the gear in it. If I need a larger pack, I just drop the fanny pack into it. When I ride horseback, I wear the fanny pack rather than put it in a saddle bag. That way, if my horse decides to go home without me, I have the emergency gear I need.

Many of the high lakes lie within the Three Sisters Wilderness Area. At this time, the Forest Service does not limit the number of people visiting the wilderness area, but you must fill out and carry with you a wilderness permit. These are available at self-service stands near the wilderness area boundary.

Visitors to wilderness areas must follow specific rules, including:

*Do not camp or build a fire* within 100 feet of a lake, stream, or trail.

*Do not secure pack or saddle stock* within 200 feet of a lake, stream, or shelter.

*Do not use mechanized equipment,* including bicycles, carts, or wheelbarrows.

*Do not camp in areas posted for rehabilitation.*

*Do not cut or damage live trees or shrubs.*

Snow blocks access to most of the lakes until late June, sometimes even later. The Forest Service district offices can tell you which lakes are believed to be open; see the *First Casts* chapter for phone numbers.

If you visit the high lakes as soon as the snow melts, you will become a walking banquet table for mosquitoes, which flourish in unbelievable abundance in damp areas. The best defenses are head nets, canvas shirts, and lots of repellent. About a month after the snow melts, the mosquito population fades from tormenting to merely annoying.

**How to Fish the High Lakes.** Fishing the high lakes is not much different than fishing any other lake. Fish are looking for the same kinds of resting places and feeding places that are described in Chapter 5.

Trout will often cruise the edges of the lakes because that is where food is found. While you may spot fish far from shore, they will usually be close to the surface feeding on hatching midges (see Chapters 5 and

South Sister from Middle Green Lake.

6) unless the lake is shallow (under 15 feet deep).

Because many of the high lakes are small, and because trout in them tend to stay near the shore, you can usually reach the fish without a rubber boat or float tube. Some anglers take the time to build a raft and paddle around the lake looking for fish, but in my opinion raft-building is an activity intended to satisfy residual boyhood urges rather than to catch fish.

Spinners are a good choice for fishing the high lakes. They can be cast a long distance and are effective for brook trout. The high elevation means most lakes will be cool, so bright spinners in sizes 1 and 2 are often suitable (see Chapter 7 for a complete discussion of spinner selection). Some of the lakes are a brownish color, and brass spinners seem to work well in them.

Bait-fishers also do well here. The fish don't usually see a lot of food and are eager for anything that looks or smells tasty. Because of timber tangles on the bottom, and the surface-oriented tendencies of the trout, fishing from the top down (see Chapter 7) with salmon eggs or worms is usually the best bait-fishing strategy. Fishing from the bottom up with Power Bait or similar bait is often not as productive because the bait can end up too deep, well below the cruising range of the fish.

Fly-fishing these lakes is rewarding, although sometimes frustrating due to limited backcast room. Good flies to carry are Adams, Elk Hair Caddis, Dougs Damselfly, Pheasant Tail Nymph, Midge Pupa, and Griffiths Gnat. Carpenter ants often are blown onto the lakes and are eaten by trout, so carry a few ant patterns. Insect hatches at these elevations are often short, but when they occur the trout go nuts and feed like there was no tomorrow.

A floating line is sufficient for most fly-fishing, although an intermediate line is occasionally useful.

When planning a trip to the high lakes, it is important to remember that the productivity of the lakes varies from one season to the next, depending on the severity of the winter. You might find a lake red-hot one summer, and dream all winter about a return trip. The next year you could find that same lake nearly barren.

**A Few of the Lakes.** There are, of course, many more lakes than those mentioned here. These are some of the larger and more popular ones.

*Bingham Lakes (elevation: 5,438 feet).* These lakes are passed on the way to Oldenberg Lake. If your interest is fishing, keep on hiking because Bingham Lakes are not stocked due to poor fish survival.

The trail begins at the Windy-Oldenberg trailhead near the southwest corner of Crescent Lake (see Chapter 2). A three-and-a-half mile hike will take you there. The terrain is not steep.

There are three small lakes and a pond in this chain. The trail passes the south-most lake, and the others are close by to the northeast. This is flat country, and that means mosquitoes.

*Blow Lake (elevation: 5,050 feet).* This is a good sized lake (55 acres) that is reached by an easy one-mile hike from a trailhead just south of Elk Lake. Fishing is good for stocked brook trout.

*Brahma Lake (elevation: 5,657 feet).* Head north on the Pacific Crest Trail (PCT) from Irish Lake; see below for directions to Irish Lake. Brahma Lake is less than three miles of easy hiking from the road. The lake is a double 12: 12 acres in size and 12 feet deep. It offers good angling for brook trout.

*Darlene Lake (elevation: 5,935 feet).* Darlene must have had a sister named Suzanne. The two lakes lie side-by-side on a trail between Windy Lakes and Oldenberg Lake (see below). They are one mile east and a bit downhill from Windy Lakes, and three miles west and a bit uphill from Oldenberg Lake.

Darlene is only 11 acres, but it can be over 40 feet deep. Fishing for brook trout can be good.

*Deer Lake (elevation: 4896 feet).* Road 4636-640 skirts the north end of Little Cultus Lake (see Chapter 2) and ends near Deer Lake. A trail goes past the lake and continues to the west end of (Big) Cultus Lake.

Deer Lake covers 70 acres, and a float tube or rubber boat could be used to reach much of it. The lake offers good fishing for medium-sized brook trout and cutthroat.

*Doris Lake (elevation: 5,320 feet).* This 90 acre lake is one mile past Blow Lake (see above). There is a little climb between the two lakes, but it doesn't qualify as "steep." The lake is deep, reaching over 70 feet. Fishing is fair for stocked brook trout.

*Farrell Lake (elevation: 5,563 feet).* Road 6010 runs from near Tandy Bay on Crescent Lake to Summit Lake. About five miles from Crescent Lake, look for the trail to Farrell and Snell lakes on the north side of the road. Farrell Lake is a half mile from the road over flat terrain. Snell Lake is just beyond it.

Small and shallow, Farrell Lake is easy to fish from shore and offers good fishing for brook trout.

*Fawn Lake (elevation: 5,632 feet).* Follow the directions to Crescent Lake (see Chapter 2). The trail leaves from the resort area. Fawn Lake is about three miles up the trail, with enough elevation gain to make you exert yourself. You can also reach the lake from Odell Lake Lodge, but it is a slightly longer hike.

Fawn Lake is about 40 acres and holds brook trout. Fishing can be good.

*Green Lakes (elevation: 6,505 feet).* The trail leads up from a developed trailhead near Sparks Lake. The climb is steady and steep for five miles, but a pretty creek lends enchantment to the sweaty effort.

The lakes are cupped in a saddle between South Sister and Broken Top. The two peaks feel close enough to touch, and the beautiful turquoise color of the lakes makes you feel like you are in another world. Take lots of film; if you can't get a good picture here, give up on photography.

There are three lakes, but at 85 acres, Middle Green dominates its two small neighbors, both of which are under 10 acres. Fishing for both rainbows and brookies can be good, but a common mistake in Middle Green is to fish too deep.

This is a very popular area—too popular as far as the Forest Service

Broken Top is visible from many of the high Cascade Lakes.

is concerned. Some day, access may be limited in order to preserve the wilderness experience.

*Hanks Lakes (elevation: 5,380 feet).* Road 4636-600 continues past Little Cultus Lake (see Chapter 2). About four miles past Little Cultus, there is a trail on the north side of the road that leads to Hanks Lakes in less than a half mile. The three lakes are each 10-15 acres. East and Middle Hanks are almost 30 feet deep, but West Hanks is about half as deep as its cousins.

East Hanks has both brookies and cutthroat, Middle Hanks is a rainbow lake, and West Hanks is brook trout only. Fishing can be quite good in any of the lakes.

*Irish Lake (elevation: 5,549 feet).* You can reach Irish Lake by car on road 4636-600 (dirt/gravel, and a bit rough). It is about six miles past Little Cultus Lake (see Chapter 2). Taylor Lake is across the road.

Irish Lake covers 28 acres and is shallow. Brook trout provide the action. Motors are not permitted.

*Kershaw Lake (elevation: 5,400 feet).* This lake is about a half mile hike past the Hanks Lakes (see above). It is only 4 acres, but can be productive for brook trout. There are a great many other small lakes in this area; all are worth a try.

*Lemish Lake (elevation: 5,155 feet).* Road 4636-600 continues past Little Cultus Lake (see Chapter 2). About two miles past Little Cultus, there is a trail on the south side of the road that leads a half mile to Lemish Lake. The trail is short, but a bit steep in the beginning.

Lemish Lake is small (14 acres), but offers good fishing for brook trout.

*Lily Lake (elevation: 5,775 feet).* This lake is reached from a side trail off the Pacific Crest Trail. Take the PCT south from its crossing at Irish and Taylor Lakes (see above for driving directions). About three miles from the trailhead there is a one-mile spur to the east that drops down to Lily Lake.

Lily Lake is small, under 15 acres, but over 40 feet deep. There are enough shoal areas, however, to keep a brook trout population going, and fishing can be good.

*Lucky Lake (elevation: 5,200 feet).* The trailhead is near the turn-off to Lava Lake. Lucky Lake is about a one-mile hike up a trail that can feel a bit steep at times. The lake is fair sized, about 30 acres, and deep. Brook trout fishing can be good.

*Meek Lake (elevation: 5,572 feet).* Road 6010 runs from near Tandy Bay on Crescent Lake to Summit Lake. About five miles from Crescent Lake, look for the Meek Lake trail on the south side of the road. The lake is a half mile from the road over flat terrain.

Meek Lake is 11 acres, with a maximum depth of almost 40 feet. Fishing is fair for brook trout and cutthroat.

*Mink Lake Basin (elevation of Mink Lake: 5,040 feet).* This lake basin can be reached in several ways, but it is a long hike no matter where you start. At 180 acres, Mink Lake is the biggest lake in the basin. It is stocked with brookies, rainbows, and cutthroat. Fishing can be good, but it is hard to get around such a large lake without a boat or float tube. Crude rafts can sometimes be found, but use extreme care if you venture out on one.

There is a shelter at Mink Lake, but it is no longer maintained, and the roof will keep out about as much rain as would a slab of Swiss cheese.

The other lakes in the basin also provide fishing, and an adventurous angler can keep busy here for quite a few days.

*Muskrat Lake (elevation: 4,850 feet).* This is one of many lakes reached on the Winopee Lake trail, which has its trailhead on the north shore of Cultus Lake (see Chapter 2). The first three-and-a-half miles lead along Cultus Lake. The resort sometimes offers shuttles (for a fee) to the west end of the lake, so you can save a little shoe leather and muscle power for later. At the west end of the lake the trail divides, with the north fork heading into a chain of lakes along Winopee Creek. Muskrat Lake is about two miles from the junction.

An old trapper's cabin is on the lake shore. It was built in the 1930s by Luther Metke, a legendary builder of log cabins. Metke finished his last cabin at Camp Sherman in 1979; he was 94 years old.

The Forest Service does not maintain shelters in the area any more, but the cabin at Muskrat Lake is kept up by a private group called "The Friends of Muskrat." You may stay in it, if you desire; just take good care of it.

Muskrat Lake is small and shallow. Fishing is fair for brook trout, rainbow, and yes, a few whitefish. There is a very nice meadow around the lake (translation: bring lots of mosquito repellent).

*Oldenberg Lake (elevation: 5,475 feet).* The west corner of Oldenberg Lake is about a mile past Bingham Lakes (see above) over level ground. Oldenberg Lake is a "30/30" lake: just under 30 acres and almost 30 feet deep. It has decent fishing for brook trout.

*Rosary Lakes (elevations: Lower Rosary, 5,707 feet; Middle Rosary, 5,830 feet; Upper Rosary, 5,835 feet).* These three lakes lie off the Pacific Crest Trail about three miles northeast of where it crosses Highway 58 at Willamette Pass. Lower Rosary is the largest lake, covering 42 acres. The other two lakes are less than 10 acres each. All three lakes are deep for their size (Lower Rosary reaches 50 feet) and hold brook trout. Lower Rosary also has rainbows and cutthroat. Fishing is good in all three lakes, but Lower Rosary has bigger fish.

*Sisters Mirror Lake (elevation: 6,000 feet).* This lake is about four miles from the trailhead at Devils Lake (see Chapter 2); the climb is steady but not steep. Sisters Mirror is one of several small lakes nestled in beautiful meadow country near South Sister. None of them is stocked, but it's worth a trip just for the scenery.

*Snell Lake (elevation: 5,612 feet).* See Farrell Lake, above, for directions. Snell Lake is under 10 acres and is shallow. Like its near neighbor Farrell Lake, it has good fishing for brook trout, with the added bonus of a few rainbows.

*Snowshoe Lakes (elevation: 5,150 feet).* These three lakes are on the Winopee Lake trail, within a mile of Winopee Lake (see Muskrat Lake and Winopee Lake for directions). Snowshoe Lake—the first one you encounter as you head north from Winopee Lake—is just under 20 acres. Middle Snowshoe is only 3 acres. At 30 acres, Upper Snowshoe is the largest of the lakes, but it is also the shallowest, only reaching 8 feet deep. All three lakes contain brook trout. Snowshoe Lake is fairly open, which makes it inviting for fly-fishers.

The junction with the Pacific Crest Trail is not far past Upper Snowshoe, near S Lake and S Creek (one wonders, is this THE S Creek, up which so many have been stuck without a paddle? But no, it derives its name from the lake, which is shaped like the letter "S").

The author scans Snowshoe Lake, looking for rising trout. His dog scans the woods, looking for squirrels to chase.

*Summit Lake (elevation: 5,553 feet).* This is a large lake (470 acres) that can be reached by car. From Crescent Lake, take road 6010 (dirt/gravel) west from near Tandy Bay. Summit Lake is about six miles distant. Due to heavy snow, the lake is often inaccessible until late June or early July. There are no special restrictions on boats. A small campground is located on the lake shore; it has tables, fire pits, and pit toilets.

Summit Lake holds brook trout, rainbows, and mackinaw. Fishing is fair. The mackinaw are like those from Cultus Lake, averaging under ten pounds.

*Suzanne Lake (elevation: 5,934 feet).* See Darlene Lake, above, for directions. Suzanne Lake covers ten acres, but is surprisingly deep (over 40 feet in places). Fishing can be pretty good for both rainbows and brook trout.

*Taylor Lake (elevation: 5,550 feet).* Taylor Lake is across the road from Irish Lake (see above for directions). At 34 acres, Taylor is a nice-sized lake, big enough to be interesting, small enough to be intimate. It is shallow (barely 10 feet deep) but not quite as productive as its neighbor Irish Lake. Still, fishing for brook trout can be good and you can reach it without a hike. Motors are not permitted.

*Teddy Lakes (elevation of South Teddy: 4,859 feet; elevation of North Teddy: 4,930 feet)*. These two lakes are on a side trail off the Winopee Lake trail (see Muskrat Lake for directions). The trail to Teddy Lakes forks off about one mile past Cultus Lake, before you reach Muskrat Lake. South Teddy is encountered almost immediately, and North Teddy is slightly beyond and higher.

Both lakes have good fishing for brook trout. North Teddy is bigger (30 acres) and deeper, and also holds rainbow trout.

*Windy Lakes (elevation: 6,200 feet)*. This chain of lakes and ponds is about four-and-a-half miles from the Windy-Oldenberg trailhead near Crescent Lake (see Chapter 2). The lakes are almost 1,400 feet higher than the trailhead, and the trail is steep in places. You should be in good shape if you want to get here.

The four main lakes range between 5 and 16 acres. The high elevation (6,200 feet) makes for a short season, so don't expect any lunkers. All the lakes contain brook trout, and South Windy Lake has some cutthroat, as well.

*Winopee Lake (elevation: 4,950 feet)*. This lake is a couple of miles past Muskrat Lake (see above) on the Winopee Lake trail. It is a pretty lake, surrounded by trees but large enough (40 acres) to let some light in. Brook trout, rainbows, and whitefish are available. Angling (especially fly-fishing) can be good if you can get through the marshy shore areas.

# 4

# The Rivers

The focus of this book is lakes, however there are two major rivers that anglers may enjoy while in the area: the Deschutes River between Wickiup Reservoir and Bend, and Fall River.

While the Deschutes starts at Little Lava Lake, I only cover it downstream from Wickiup Dam. Between Little Lava Lake and Crane Prairie, the Deschutes is a small, shallow stream that is only open in June, July, and August. Prior to June the river is closed to protect spawning rainbows, and after August it is closed to protect spawning brook trout and kokanee. During the open season, you may find an occasional small fish, but pickings are generally slim.

Below Wickiup, however, the Deschutes is a big river with big trout, both rainbows and browns, and an abundant whitefish population. Fishing season on this stretch is the same as for the lakes in the area.

Fall River is fly-fishing-only water, and one of the prettiest places you could wish to fish. Even though the trout are small, it's a good place to make an occasional visit.

## Deschutes River

Below Wickiup Dam, the Deschutes is broad and fairly uniform in depth. The banks are accessible and public in many stretches, although you must watch carefully to avoid wandering onto private land.

The river channel is public, however, and as long as you stay in the water you are not trespassing. Almost any kind of craft can be used in most of the river, but NO kind of craft should be used in the areas where there are falls and rapids. The falls, rapids, and log jams are not passable, and extreme caution and judgment should be used when near them. In the summer of 1993, four people drowned in three separate accidents on this stretch of river. All of these tragedies were preventable.

One word of caution for those boating the flat sections of the river: be careful how you anchor. This was forcefully brought home to me the

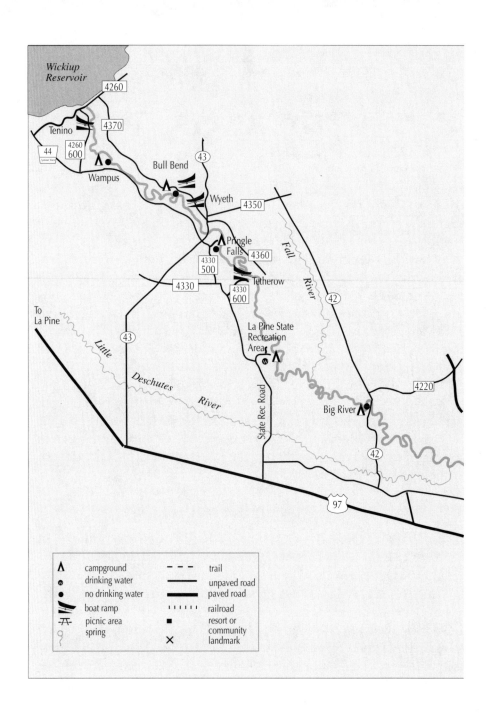

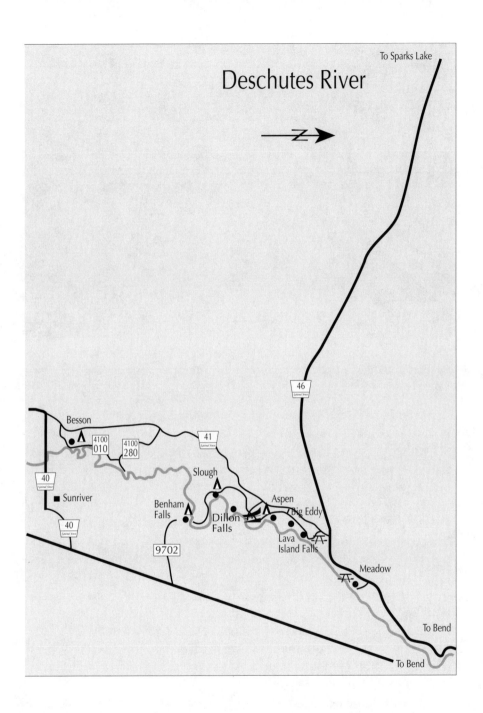

Deschutes River

To Sparks Lake

Besson

4100 010

4100 280

41

46

40

Sunriver

40

Slough

Benham Falls

9702

Dillon Falls

Aspen

Big Eddy

Lava Island Falls

Meadow

To Bend

To Bend

There are two foot bridges over the upper Deschutes River: this one above Benham Falls, and another at Besson Camp. The latter is for the use of guests of Sunriver Resort.

first time I visited here. I came with two friends—Jack, who brought his boat, and Mike, who supplied the outboard motor. On our last day, Mike plied the west bank of the river, while I worked the east bank. Jack took the boat and fished down the middle. He'd fish a bit, then drift his boat to a new spot, let down the anchor, and fish some more.

The flaw in Jack's strategy was that he tied the anchor line firmly to the stern of the boat. This worked fine for a while, but then the anchor snagged on an underwater boulder in fast water. The push of current pulled the stern down, and water poured over the transom. Jack dove for the bow, trying to level the boat before it swamped. He saved the boat, but now he was in the bow, while the anchor cleat was 14 feet behind him.

Jack was stuck in mid-river, certain he'd sink his boat and lose all his fishing gear. Mike stood on one shore figuring out how he was going to recover his motor after the boat sank. I found the spectacle amusing, but then I didn't own anything that was about to sink.

By extremely careful balancing of his body weight, and incredible stretching of his arms, Jack reached the anchor line and loosened it. The boat drifted free. Luckily, Jack is a tall man. If his arms had been two inches shorter, he'd have become a swimmer.

The moral is, be careful where you anchor, and always let out enough line to keep the boat balanced. And never tie down the anchor line until you are sure you are safe.

Flies, spinners, spoons, plugs, and bait all work well in this river. When the sun is bright, the trout tend to hunker on the bottom, next to grassy banks, or under logs.

Spinners and spoons cast near the bank and retrieved slowly are a good tactic. Another approach is to cast your lure upstream so that it will have time to sink near the bottom when it is across from you. Then let the current swing it around until it is directly downstream.

Dry-fly fishing can be productive next to grassy banks and behind logs. September and October are especially good months. Elk Hair Caddis and Adams are usually effective patterns.

Nymphs fished deep can also catch fish, as can streamers such as Zonkers, Muddler Minnows, and Matuka-style flies. The streamers can produce well when fished next to undercut banks and logs, and when fished deep on a sinking line. In the latter case, cast across and slightly downstream and let the current swing the fly around; or while drifting slowly downstream, cast to the bank and retrieve the fly.

A good bait-fishing technique is to use a sliding-sinker rig like that described for fishing from the bottom-up in Chapter 7. Use a night-crawler for bait and cast downstream into slow water near steep banks. Slowly reel in. This works well, but resign yourself to losing a lot of hooks and sinkers on snags.

**Access.** Road 4370 is a one-and-a-half-lane dirt and gravel road that follows the northwest bank of the Deschutes from Wickiup Dam to above Pringle Falls. There are many places to stop and fish along this road, and some of them are suitable for camping if you are self-contained. Road 4370 is not always next to the river, but several spur roads lead there. These include 4370-020 (which goes to the Wyeth boat ramp described below), -030, -050, and -070. Bull Bend Campground is on 4370-092.

Road 4260-600 is a short single-lane dirt road on the southeast shore opposite road 4370. It starts near Wickiup Dam: go between the salmon-pink maintenance buildings and a blocked road to the spillway. Where 4260-600 is away from the river, there are often spurs that lead to the bank; these spurs can be quite rough, however. Tenino Boat Ramp is on this road. Downstream from it, most of the riverbank is private property.

Road 4260-600 links up to road 44 a couple of miles from the dam.

Road 44 is two-lane gravel here and passes near the southeast bank beginning about three miles below Wickiup dam. Where road 44 is away from the Deschutes, there are dirt spurs that go to the river. One of these leads to Wampus Campground; there is a sign for it on road 44.

Road 42 crosses the Deschutes at Big River Campground, but offers no other river access.

Road 43 crosses the Deschutes near Pringle Falls. The Pringle Falls Campground is not at this crossing, however. To reach it, take road 4330-500 (there is a sign for Pringle Falls Campground and Tetherow Boat Ramp). You soon turn right onto 4330-600, then proceed a half mile to the campground.

The Tetherow boat ramp is below Pringle Falls Campground on road 4330-500. There is a sign for it on road 43. Another way to get there is to take 4330 where it crosses road 43, then follow 4330-600, a one-and-a-half-lane dirt road, one mile to the launch.

Below the Tetherow ramp, the next access is at the big (I mean, BIG) La Pine State Recreation Area. The best way to reach it is from the east on State Rec Road, which intersects US 97 about 21 miles south of Bend and seven miles north of La Pine. There is a sign on US 97.

Below the State Recreation Area, the Deschutes flows through private property most of the way to Big River Campground.

Below Big River Campground, most river access is off road 41. This two-lane gravel road runs between roads 40 (near Sunriver resort) and 46 (near Inn of the Seventh Mountain resort). There is no sign on road 40 to indicate its junction with road 41, but there is a sign that says "Mt. Bachelor JCT 2 Miles;" the road 41 junction is at this sign.

The first access off road 41 is down road 4100-200. There is a sign for "Besson Camp" at the intersection. Go 1.3 miles down this two-lane gravel road to reach the river at Besson Camp. The road becomes single-lane dirt and continues another three-quarters mile along the river, eventually joining road 4100-280 (described below). After the first quarter mile, a fenced (but not posted) pasture is between the road and the river. There is a stile over the fence that allows access to the river.

Road 4100-280 intersects road 41 3.7 miles past the Besson Camp turn-off, just opposite the seven mile marker. After a quarter mile, the road forks. Take the right fork; the left leads to a quarry and does not offer river access. Road 4100-280 continues another 2.5 miles to the

This fishing platform is for the use of those who are handicapped. It is located where road 42 crosses the Deschutes.

river. There is a bridge over the Deschutes here. It is for the use of guests of Sunriver resort.

Road 4120 intersects road 41 between mile markers 2 and 3. There is a sign for "Dillon Falls/Slough Camp/Benham Falls." After a half mile the road splits. Slough Camp and Benham Falls are to the right, 1.7 and 3.0 miles respectively, down road 4120-100. After Slough Camp, road 4120-100 is not suited to trailers.

Meanwhile, back at the fork, a left turn takes you down 4120-490 to Dillon Falls. There is a boat ramp here. DO NOT GO DOWNSTREAM!

The next river access is from road 4120-500. There is a sign on 41 for "Big Eddy/Aspen." The road soon Ts; go right 0.4 miles down 4120 to reach the Aspen boat ramp, or left 0.5 miles to reach Big Eddy.

The last access off road 41 is to Lava Island Falls. There is a sign on 41 that puts you on road 4120. After a half mile, 4120 forks. The left fork offers the best access to the river.

Road 4600-100 intersects road 46 1.2 miles east of the Inn of the Seventh Mountain resort. Proceed 0.8 miles down this road to reach Meadow Picnic Area.

Road 9702 heads west from US 97 and ends at the Benham Falls recreation site.

**Campgrounds and Recreation Sites.** With the exception of the La Pine State Recreation Area, all the campgrounds on the Deschutes are primitive Forest Service sites and offer few amenities. None of these has drinking water or trash pickup, and none has a fee.

*Tenino Boat Ramp.* This concrete ramp is the first place you can put in below Wickiup Dam. It is OK to camp here, but there are no facilities at all.

*Wampus Campground.* One of the more obscure campgrounds in the area, Wampus offers a single unisex pit toilet and occasional flat places to camp. That's it.

*Bull Bend.* One good flood and this will be a boat-in campground. It is located where the river makes a 180 degree turn. The road into the campground is on a narrow neck of land, and you can see the river on either side of the road. There is a message board at the road junction. Bull Bend is a reduced service campground with tables, fire pits, pit toilets, and a gravel boat ramp near the entrance.

*Wyeth Campground.* Wyeth offers a boat ramp, a pit toilet, and one table. You may camp here if you can find a level patch of ground; good luck. This is the last boat ramp before Pringle Falls. Don't attempt to float Pringle Falls. Period.

*Pringle Falls Campground.* The campground is on road 4400-500, a single-lane dirt road. The campground is small and offers only a few tables, some decrepit fire pits, and a pit toilet. The nearest boat ramp is the Tetherow launch.

*Tetherow Boat Ramp.* This is a concrete boat ramp with limited trailer parking. It puts you in the river below Pringle Falls and Tetherow log jam. The roads leading to Tetherow are rough; you really have to want to get here.

*La Pine State Recreation Area.* This huge park has 95 full-hookup RV camp sites and another 50 sites with electricity, table, fire pit, and water. Facilities include restrooms with showers, day-use area, and a sanitary dump. Overnight fees are $14 or $15 per night. The recreation area borders the west bank of the Deschutes and the south bank of Fall River.

*Big River Campground.* The "Big" refers to the river, not the campground, which is quite small. It is where road 42 crosses the Deschutes. There is a concrete boat ramp across road 42 from the campground, but trailer parking is limited.

*Besson Campground.* This camp is at the end of road 4100-200. It

Most of the upper Deschutes is placid, but every so often the river plunges down a raging, impassable cataract like this one at Benham Falls.

provides a concrete boat ramp, pit toilets, and one table.

*Benham Falls (West)*. Road 4120-100 ends here. You can walk 200 feet to get a nice view of the falls, or walk up an old railroad grade five-eighths mile to the river above the falls. There is a bridge here that takes you into Benham Falls Picnic Area (see below).

*Benham Falls (East)*. Road 9702, which departs from US 97 near the Lava Lands Visitors Center, takes you to this picnic area. There are tables and a boat launch, but no drinking water or camping.

*Slough Camp.* A concrete boat ramp, a few scattered tables, and a pit toilet—that's all you get at Slough Camp. You can launch here and ply the river between Benham Falls and Dillon Falls; there is a take out above Dillon Falls. DO NOT, under any circumstances, attempt to boat Dillon Falls. They are extremely dangerous.

*Dillon Falls.* There is a boat ramp here. DO NOT go downstream!

*Aspen.* This is a dirt boat ramp reached on road 4120. There are no other facilities here.

*Big Eddy.* You can park here and walk to the river. The Lava Island Falls rapids are here, but there is fishing along the banks nearby.

*Lava Island Falls.* This is a day-use area with pit toilets equipped for the handicapped.

*Meadow Picnic Area.* This is another day-use area with tables and pit toilets. It is at the end of road 4600-100.

**Fishing Regulations.** Open from the fourth Saturday in April to October 31. Up to five trout per day may be kept, with a six-inch minimum and no more than two brown trout. Only one trout over 20 inches may be kept. There is no limit on whitefish. From September 1 to October 31, there is an additional closure from Wickiup Dam downstream about a quarter mile to the cable crossing.

**Boating Regulations.** Between Wickiup Dam and the National Forest boundary, the regulations call for a 5 mph maximum speed and no wake. Motors are not permitted downstream from the National Forest Boundary until you reach Jefferson County (many miles north).

## Fall River

This is one of the most beautiful streams in Central Oregon, the kind of place where you often hear comments like, "No, I didn't catch anything, but with water this pretty, who cares?"

Fall River is a fly-fishing-only stream. It emerges without preamble, springing from the rocks and becoming a full-fledged river within a few hundred yards. It flows crystal clear for eight miles through stands of lodgepole and mature ponderosa pine before merging with the Deschutes.

Fly-fishers have always had a passion for spring creeks such as Fall River. The shallow, transparent water whispers "dry fly! cast a dry fly!" to every long-rod angler who ventures to its banks. It's a rare day that

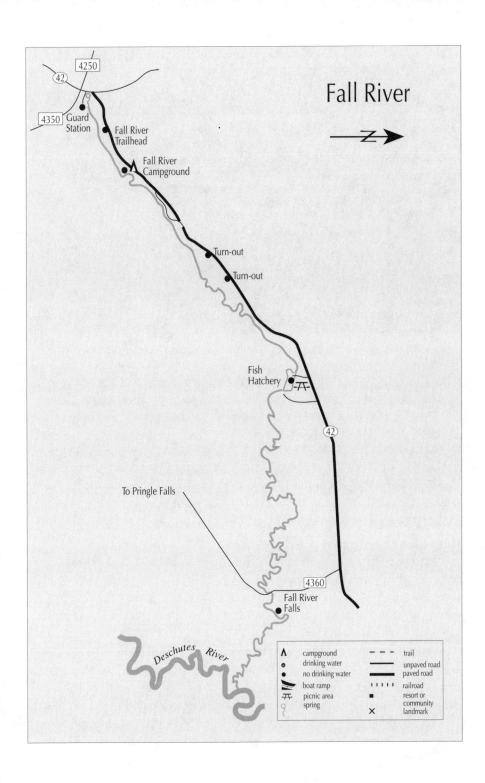

Fall River

4250

42

4350 Guard
Station

Fall River
Trailhead

Fall River
Campground

Turn-out

Turn-out

Fish
Hatchery

42

To Pringle Falls

4360

Fall River
Falls

Deschutes River

| | | | |
|---|---|---|---|
| ∧ campground | | – – – trail | |
| ⊙ drinking water | | unpaved road | |
| ● no drinking water | | paved road | |
| boat ramp | | ׀ ׀ ׀ ׀ railroad | |
| ⊼ picnic area | | ■ resort or | |
| ♀ spring | | community | |
| | | ✕ landmark | |

An angler fishes a mayfly hatch on Fall River above the hatchery.

you don't find a half dozen hopeful fly-fishers drifting a Thorax Pale Morning Dun or a Parachute Adams on the popular stretches.

You have to pick your fishing water carefully here. The upper reach of the river is beautiful, but has few fish. The best stretches are near the hatchery, where the water is deeper and there are some ledges, and below the falls. Above the falls, this is a rainbow fishery. Downstream from the falls, an occasional brown trout comes up from the Deschutes. Be aware, however, that after September 30, the river is closed to angling from the falls to the Deschutes in order to protect spawning brown trout.

Because the river lacks depth and rocks, fish make do with whatever cover they can find. During a hatch, you will spot rising fish on the flats, but the rest of the time they will be next to grassy banks, under downed logs, behind ledges, under whitewater, and in deep water, where it exists.

This is demanding fishing. The clear water combined with a lack of cover makes for shy fish. Long leaders with thin tippets (12 feet tapered to 6X, if your casting and your rod can handle it) are needed. Because the water is shallow, the trout will usually rise to a dry fly.

Some spring creeks, like Idaho's famous Silver Creek, are incredibly productive waters, with massive insect hatches and thousands of big, wild trout. But Fall River, for all its beauty, is not a rich stream. The water is cold and there are not enough depth or nutrients to nurture the robust biomass that big trout require. Other than an occasional brown trout below the falls, these are small hatchery rainbows, and anything over ten inches is a big fish. Still, with water this pretty, who cares?

**Access.** The river is only eight miles long, with a state fish hatchery at about the mid-point. Above the hatchery, most of the river bank is public land, while below the hatchery, most land is private.

Road 42 parallels the river from its origin to the fish hatchery, and all of this bank has public access. The Fall River Trail starts at the upper end of the river and goes down the north bank as far as the hatchery.

Downstream from the fish hatchery until the river joins the Deschutes, much of the south bank is within the La Pine State Recreation Area, but most of the north bank is private property.

The mileages shown below are measured along road 42 from its junction with roads 4250 and 4350.

0.1     Guard Station. You can park here and walk to the beginnings of Fall River where it bubbles out of the ground. This is not a good place to fish, but it is intriguing nonetheless.

0.5     Roadside turn-out. The river is about 100 yards below the turn-out. The Fall River Trail starts here and proceeds down the north bank as far as the fish hatchery.

0.8     Fall River Campground. A sign on road 42 directs you onto the gravel road that enters the campground. This riverbank campground is small, with no designated sites and limited facilities. There are tables, fire pits, and pit toilets, but no trash dumpsters or drinking water. There is no fee. A day-use area with tables and fire pits is located near the entry. The campground is a good place to pick up the Fall River Trail.

1.2     Spur road. The road crosses the Fall River Trail and leads to the river, then follows it for less than a half mile.

1.6     Spur road. This is the other end of the road described above.

2.0     Turn-out. You may park here and walk down to the river.

2.8     Turn-out. Park here. The river is down the hill and across a grassy flat.

3.8     Fish Hatchery. There is a sign on 42 for the ODFW fish hatchery.

Turn onto the gravel road and park in the visitors area. There are picnic tables on the grass near here. The green lawns and old brown hatchery buildings with their white trim and red roofs give a gentle, rural feel, and grounds look more like a park than a fish hatchery.

Walk across the lawn to the river and fish anywhere along the bank, but keep in mind that people live here. The Fall River Trail provides upstream access.

4.0    Fall River Drive. This road leads to private property and does not offer access to the river.

5.7    Road 4360. This is a gravel road that leads to the river in 0.7 miles. There are parking areas near the bridge on both sides of the river. For upstream access, there is a dirt road on the south bank that parallels the river for a quarter mile; the north bank is too boggy for good upstream access. Downstream, there is a trail on the north side of the river; the south side is too brushy for good access.

The best place to pick up the downstream trail is from the parking area north of the bridge. The Fall River falls is downstream about a quarter mile. Below the falls, Fall River is closed to angling after September 30. About a mile below the falls the river joins the Deschutes.

There is no road access to Fall River below road 4360. There are several spur roads off 42 between this point and where 42 crosses the Deschutes at Big River Campground (7.8 miles from road 4250), but none of them lead to Fall River.

**Fishing Regulations.** Open from the fourth Saturday in April to October 31, except below the falls where the season closes after September 30. Fly-angling with barbless hooks only. Up to five trout per day may be kept, with a six-inch minimum. No more than one fish over 20 inches may be kept. There is no limit on whitefish.

**Boating Regulations.** Fall River is not a navigable body of water.

# 5

# Fishing the Cascade Lakes

Good lake fishing tactics mean being in the right place, at the right depth, presenting something attractive to fish without arousing their defensive instincts.

These five elements—place, depth, presentation, attraction, and stealth—are described in Chapters 5-7. Place, depth, and stealth are discussed in this chapter after a description of the primary Cascade Lakes game fish; catch-and-release fishing is covered at the chapter's end. Presentation and attraction are covered in Chapter 6 (fly-fishing) and Chapter 7 (fishing with bait and lures).

## Understanding the Fish

**Rainbow Trout.** Rainbows are prized for their beauty and their acrobatics when hooked. They are native to the rivers of western America, but adapt well when stocked in lakes. Most of the rainbows in the Cascade Lakes are from the Oak Springs hatchery on the Deschutes River, however some fish are now being planted from a Klamath Lake strain.

Both strains feed primarily on aquatic insects, leeches, and crustaceans such as crayfish, snails, and scuds. Larger fish will eat small fish

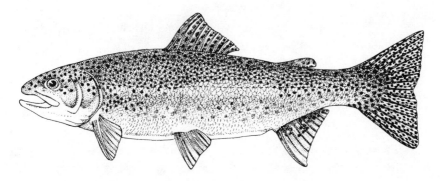

Rainbow Trout (drawing courtesy ODFW)

such as chub and whitefish when they are available, but the Klamath strain seems more inclined to do so.

Rainbows have a life span of six or seven years, and reach a size that depends on the amount of food available. A rich environment like Crane Prairie Reservoir can grow a six-pound rainbow in four years.

Like all true trout, rainbows need running water to reproduce and seek an inlet or outlet stream for their spring spawning run. If they don't find one, they will spawn anyway, but the eggs won't survive.

**Brown Trout.** Brown trout are native to Europe, where people have angled for them since before the time of Julius Caesar. It appears that all the stupid ones were caught many centuries ago, and by the time they were imported to the United States in the late 19th century, they had a well-deserved reputation for being hard to catch.

Browns are adaptable fish. In general, their oxygen needs are less than that of other trout species, which means they can survive in warmer water. They have been known to eat everything from size 28 midges to ducklings. Within that size range, any animal that swims, crawls, burrows, drifts, alights or otherwise lives in or on water, is in danger of being eaten by a brown trout.

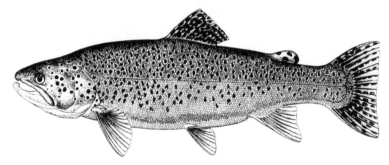

Brown Trout (drawing courtesy ODFW)

This adaptability in appetite and habitat, combined with their natural wariness, has allowed brown trout to thrive in a variety of aquatic environments. Because they live long, they can grow to very large size, as demonstrated at Paulina Lake in 1993 when a 27 pound brown set the Oregon state record.

Browns spawn in the fall, but, like rainbows, they require running water for the spawn to be successful. They cannot find the right conditions in East and Paulina lakes, but those in Wickiup migrate to Browns Creek, Sheep Springs, and the Deschutes River to lay their eggs. Below

Wickiup, Deschutes River browns spawn in the Deschutes and in the lower reaches of Fall River and Spring River.

**Brook Trout.** Brook trout are not actually trout. They are a member of the char family, a group that also includes bull trout and mackinaw. Furthermore, nobody out West calls running water a "brook." But somehow the name "crick char" never caught on.

As you might suspect, brook trout are another import, this time from eastern North America. A particularly hardy fish, brookies can survive in a harsh environment that is marginal for fish production. For this reason, they are the most commonly stocked fish in the high lakes.

Brook trout don't get as big as other trout in the lakes, even with rich feed, and a 20 inch brookie is a trophy. Brook trout have a diet similar to that of rainbows, except they are not prone to eat other fish. Even so, they will often take a streamer fly or spinner.

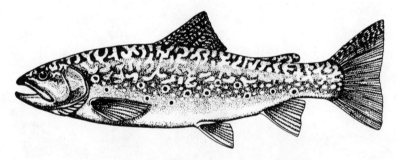

Brook Trout (drawing courtesy ODFW)

The easiest time to catch brook trout is in the spring. They are very aggressive just after the ice melts, and are receptive to bait, surface flies and lures. By summer, however, they hunker down on the bottom and become hard to catch. When fall comes, they resume their receptivity.

Brookies are a colorful fish, especially so when their hues intensify in the fall spawning season. Unlike brown trout and rainbows, they can reproduce in either running water, lakes, or cold up-welling spring water. This is sometimes a problem since they can over-reproduce and exceed their food supply, resulting in a population of stunted fish with big heads and small bodies. Under these circumstances, catch-and-cook fishing can improve the balance between the fish and their food supply.

**Kokanee.** Kokanee are a land-locked sockeye salmon. In Oregon, they are native to Wallowa and Suttle Lakes, where geologic forces isolated them from the ocean and forced their adaptation to still waters. They are a popular fish in the Cascade Lakes, and good sport on the right tackle. And they are the best tasting fish you can catch here.

The primary diet of kokanee is plankton (microscopic plants and animals) which they strain from the water with their gillrakers. However, they will strike spoons and other lures, and sometimes even take bait. They can be found at many depths, even 80 feet or more.

Kokanee may be a salmon, but because they are cut off from the rich ocean feeding grounds, they don't grow to large size. A typical Cascade Lakes kokanee is nine to thirteen inches long, and a fish over 18 inches is rare.

Kokanee are fall spawners. Fish that are ready to spawn develop red bodies and green heads, and you can often see a school of them cavorting on the surface, cruising the shallows, and generally acting silly. (It's reassuring to realize that man is not the only animal that behaves like a fool when sexually aroused.)

Kokanee need running water for successful spawning. Therefore in some of the Cascade Lakes, such as Odell, Elk, and Wickiup, kokanee are self-sustaining. In other lakes they are stocked. Like all Pacific salmon, kokanee die after spawning.

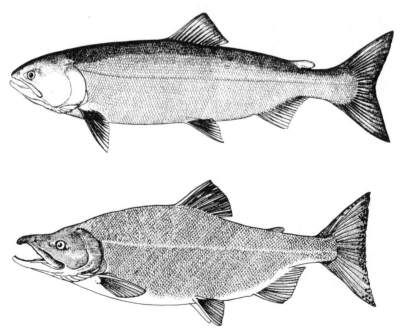

Pre-spawning kokanee (top) and male kokanee during spawning.
(drawings courtesy ODFW)

**Coho Salmon.** Coho salmon from Sandy River stock are a newcomer to the Cascade Lakes. At this time, they are planted only in Wickiup Reservoir, where they seem to be adapting well to still-water living.

Coho begin life as insect eaters, with a diet similar to rainbow trout. Later they switch to a fish diet. They live to be about three years old before they spawn, and usually weigh about three pounds when mature. They die after their fall spawning run.

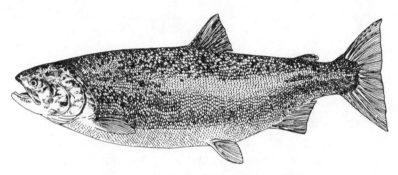

Coho Salmon (drawing courtesy ODFW)

**Atlantic Salmon.** As you might expect, these fish are not native to western America. They were planted in Hosmer Lake in 1958, and for many years that was the only place west of the Mississippi where they were successfully established.

ODFW has experimented with different strains of these fish, and the ones currently being stocked are not as large nor as surface-oriented as an earlier strain. They eat both insects and other fish, and it is believed that larger Atlantics (those over 16 inches) will forage on troublesome chub populations in East and Davis Lakes.

Atlantics live for six to eight years and can grow to around 20 inches. They tend to be acrobatic when hooked and can make spectacular leaps. They attempt to spawn in the fall, but without running water the

Atlantic Salmon (drawing courtesy ODFW)

spawn do not survive. Unlike cohos and kokanee, Atlantic salmon do not die after spawning.

**Mackinaw.** Mackinaw, also known as lake trout, are deep-dwelling fish that feed on other fish. They grow slowly, but live long, adding about a pound a year. Twenty-pound fish are not uncommon. Because mackinaw are big and eat other fish, they are caught on large lures and flies.

These fish are tolerant of cold water, preferring temperatures of 48-52 degrees. They are often found at great depths, and it is not unusual to catch one on the bottom in 150 feet of water. However, in the spring when the lake surface is cool, they can be found in shallow water and have been known to take big streamer flies.

Mackinaw spawn in the fall; like brook trout, they can reproduce in still water.

Mackinaw are sometimes confused with bull trout, a protected species in Oregon. If you catch a fish you suspect is a mackinaw, examine it carefully to make sure it is not a bull trout. Bull trout have a greenish skin color, where mackinaw are gray. Also, a mackinaw's tail is more deeply forked.

Mackinaw (top) and bull trout (bottom)
(drawings courtesy ODFW)

# Where to Fish

In the future, anglers may have the option of buying an electronic fish finder. I don't mean one of those crude gizmos we have today that only tells you when a fish is underneath you, but a real finder. This sophisticated device would tell you the precise coordinates and depth of every fish in the lake, along with its species and what lure it is most receptive to. Then the fish finder would steer your boat to the best fish, tie on the right lure, cast it, and reel in the fish. After the finder has netted the fish for you, its computerized voice will brag about its catch, even adding a few inches to the length.

Until we reach that high-tech future (and I'd take up golf before I'd "fish" like that), anglers must rely on their understanding of fish behavior before they can find their quarry. This is not easy. Many anglers look at the blank surface of a big lake and panic. "The fish could be anywhere!" they think. This panic comes from looking at the entire lake at one time. The trick is to break the big problem ("how do I find a fish in a million cubic feet of water") into smaller pieces, then solve each piece. This means estimating where the fish are in general, then finding where they are in particular.

If you understand a fish's basic needs (discussed below), you can scan a lake and pick several likely spots to fish. Since we fish in three dimensions, not two, positioning yourself on the surface of the lake only solves part of the problem. The other part—depth—is discussed later in this chapter. Once you are positioned in the general neighborhood of fish and have chosen a depth to present your offering, you can start searching a smaller area to find where the fish are in particular. You do this by casting, trolling, or re-positioning yourself in the general area. If one area does not produce, move on and try another.

**What Fish Need.** Fish have four simple concerns: food, safety, comfort, and, at certain times of the year, spawning. Understanding how fish satisfy these needs, and how these needs differ for each species, is the key to finding receptive fish.

*Food.* Fish in lakes generally take their food where it is produced. This is different than fish in rivers, who usually feed where the current concentrates the food. For fish in a river, eating is like going to a drive-in restaurant: you park in a good spot and wait for dinner to be brought to you. But lake fish tend to cruise a small area looking for the food du jour and slurping it down when they see it. If you understand what critters are eaten by lake-dwelling fish, and where those critters are found, you are a long ways towards finding fish. Chapter 6 summarizes what fish eat in lakes.

*Safety.* From the moment they are born, fish in the Cascade Lakes have many predators. These include: herons, gulls, and osprey, who strike from above, grabbing fish that are near the surface or in shallow water; otters and cormorants, who swim through the water and pick off unwary fish; other fish; and humans. When fish are not feeding, they rest in a safe place. Even when they feed, they want a safe haven nearby.

*Comfort.* Oxygen and temperature are the keys to fish comfort. Fish require oxygen, which they extract from the water with their gills. Water holds oxygen in inverse proportion to temperature, so the warmer the water, the less oxygen it contains. Different species of fish have different tolerances to low oxygen in the water. Rainbow trout require lots of oxygen, but bass require much less. This is why in the summer you find bass in the south end of Crane Prairie Reservoir (where the water is warmer), and trout in the north end where cool water flows into the lake.

There is a flip side to temperature, however. Fish are cold-blooded, and low temperatures slow their metabolism. The response to cold temperatures, like the response to oxygen, varies with fish species. Some, like whitefish, are more tolerant than others. This is one reason why whitefish are more easily caught than trout when the water is cold (below 50 degrees).

*Spawning.* Fish of all species attempt to spawn when they are mature, even those whose spawn will perish due to a lack of running water. Understanding which species spawn at which season, and what kind of water they will seek, can be a key to solving the "where are the fish in general" problem.

**Positioning Yourself on the Lake.** When you first come to a new lake, take a few minutes to look around. If you see rising trout, you've found some, but maybe not all, active fish. It's easy to be distracted by rising fish. They're so tantalizing, so visually arousing, and you know where they are. But those rise rings rippling across the surface can be a siren's song luring you to hours of frustrated fishing.

Take a hard squint at those rising fish. How big are they? If they are little fish that come half way out of the water, they are probably chub, a five-inch trash fish. They may be juvenile trout, another opportunity you can afford to pass up. They may be decent-sized trout, but the big ones may be feeding subsurface where you can't see them. Or they could be five-pound rainbows slurping mayflies. In any case, try to understand what you are seeing before rushing over.

After you've scanned the water for rising fish, look for food concentrations. Some likely places are:

*Weed beds.* These are the primary areas for growing the aquatic insects that fish eat.

*Shallow areas with good exposure to the sun,* especially in early season. Usually, this means places that face west or south.

*Coves and bays that are protected from strong wave action.* These provide better growing areas for aquatic vegetation, allowing insect life to proliferate. In the Cascade Lakes, the strongest winds come from the southwest, so look for areas protected from those winds.

*Gentle slopes.* These allow vegetation and other insect habitat to accumulate.

*Down timber.* A good place for caddis larvae, leeches, scuds, and the nymphs of dragonflies and damselflies.

*Silty areas.* These often support midge larvae.

*Places with current.* Yes, even lakes can have current. Inlet streams, outlet streams (including dam spillways), and old river channels in reservoirs such as Wickiup and Crane Prairie can create currents that gather food for fish.

*Along windward shores.* Smaller food such as midge pupae can be blown towards the shore and concentrated there. However, a more important consideration for predators like brown trout is that windy areas collect baitfish.

Now that you've spotted some food concentrations, identify resting

Gentle slopes allow vegetation and trout food to accumulate.

places—places where fish can satisfy their safety and comfort needs. Some resting places are:

*Near inlet areas;* they bring cooler, oxygenated water to the lake.

*Deep water* (safety from overhead predators and, to some extent, cooler water).

*Shady places* (less light reaching the water means fish are harder for a predator to see).

*Among down or standing timber* (hiding places from predators).

*Within weed beds, under floating weeds,* etc. (hiding places).

*Beneath overhead cover* such as floating logs (safety from overhead predators). Wind-riffle and wave chop are also forms of overhead cover that make fish feel more secure.

*Among an underwater boulder field* (hiding places).

*Near underwater springs* (cooler, oxygenated water; or, if it is a hot spring, warmth in the early season).

Now, look for the best combinations of resting places and food concentrations. That's where you want to start fishing. An area that has both food and safety in one place is ideal, but this combination is not often found. More often, fish will feed in areas that have safety nearby, such

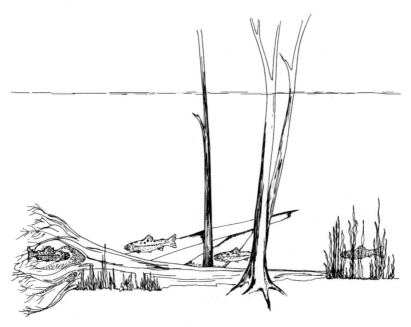

Down timber and standing snags are good habitat for many foods that fish eat. They also provide hiding places for fish.

as a gentle slope near a drop-off. The gentle slope offers food, while the drop-off offers a quick exit to safety.

The biggest, most aggressive fish will be found in the very best places. In the case of a drop-off near a gentle slope, you will find the biggest fish closest to the drop-off. Another example is the overhead cover offered by a floating log; the largest fish will usually be found where the water is deepest beneath the log.

Keep in mind that the "best places" will change with the hour or weather. If it is overcast, fish might feel safe at noon in water they would shun on a sunny day. Also, a little wind riffle makes surface feeding fish feel more secure, and thus more receptive to a lure or fly.

Another thing to remember is that lakes change. This year's lunker alley might be next year's dullsville because the lake level went up (or down), or the balance of food shifted to another species. Smart lake anglers constantly re-evaluate the waters they fish and don't get stuck in the rut of fishing the same part of the lake the same way, year after year.

Recognize, too, that some general movements of fish are predictable based on season. For instance, fish are often found in the shallows in spring because that is where sunlight first warms the water and generates insect activity. By summer, however, warm water temperatures and

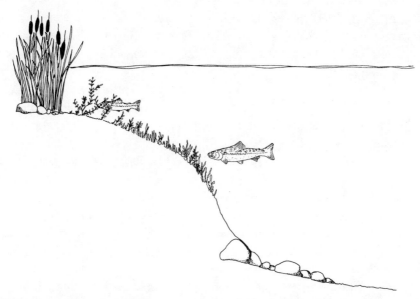

A drop-off near a gentle slope is an ideal place for big fish: they get abundant food and a handy exit to safety.

heavy fishing pressure can cause the fish to seek deeper water. When fall arrives, they will start back to the shallows.

Spawning migrations are also predictable general trends. Brown trout and kokanee start heading for the creeks in the fall, and brook trout will move into the shallows. Rainbows, on the other hand, spawn in the spring before the fishing season opens. However, in early season they often are found near the tributary creeks where they spawned, lingering until warmer water stirs them into active pursuit of food.

## How Deep to Fish

Positioning yourself on the surface of the lake takes care of two of the three dimensions. Next, you have to decide how deep to fish. Like everything else about lake fishing, the answer depends on many factors, and water temperature is one of the biggest.

During most of the fishing season in the Cascade Lakes, the water gets colder as you go deeper. Some of the deeper lakes will stratify in the summer. That is, the warmer water is on top, and the temperature declines slowly with depth. Then it drops quickly in a transition zone called the thermocline. Below the thermocline, the temperature decreases more slowly, but the thermocline forms a barrier below which oxygen and nutrients don't easily pass.

As mentioned earlier, the ability of water to contain oxygen increases as the water gets colder. Therefore, fish are often found just above the thermocline (in lakes that stratify) because that is where they can get the most oxygen.

In lakes that don't stratify, fish are often found near the bottom where the water is coldest. However, in very rich lakes, fish will not rest right on the bottom because decaying vegetation sucks oxygen out of the water.

A fish's search for oxygen is balanced by its cold-blooded metabolism, which lowers with decreasing temperature. Trout in the Cascade Lakes seem to prefer water between 50 and 68 degrees. Below 50 degrees, they start slowing down, becoming poor feeders, and your chances of catching them diminish. Above 68 degrees, fish become more concerned with satisfying their oxygen needs than with the pursuit of food.

Water temperature plays such a big role in fish behavior that I always carry two thermometers with me when I visit a lake. One is a traditional glass tube that I use to take surface readings. The other is a small

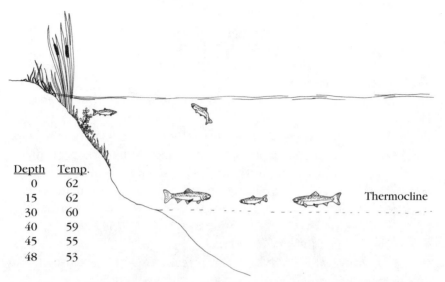

| Depth | Temp. |
|-------|-------|
| 0 | 62 |
| 15 | 62 |
| 30 | 60 |
| 40 | 59 |
| 45 | 55 |
| 48 | 53 |

Thermocline

In a deep lake that stratifies, water temperature declines slowly with depth, then drops rapidly through the thermocline. Below the thermocline, temperature declines more slowly, but oxygen and nutrients don't pass through. Fish are found above the thermocline but not below it.

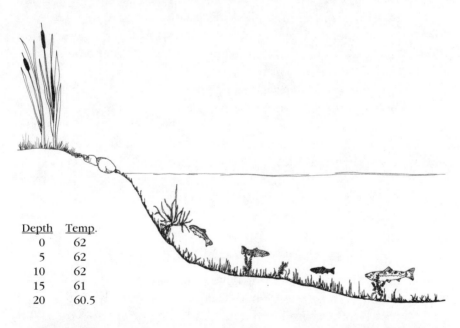

| Depth | Temp. |
|-------|-------|
| 0 | 62 |
| 5 | 62 |
| 10 | 62 |
| 15 | 61 |
| 20 | 60.5 |

In an unstratified lake there is no thermocline, and fish are found at whatever depth gives them the best combination of food, safety, and comfort.

electronic affair with a temperature probe on a 50 foot wire. I dangle the probe in the water and take readings at various depths. By using these two thermometers, I can find out where the thermocline is (if there is one), make some guesses about how active the fish are, judge the likelihood of insect activity, and so forth.

Temperature is not the only factor that determines how deep fish will be found. Some others are:

*The amount of light reaching the fish.* This depends on both the clarity of the water and the intensity of the sunlight, the latter being a function of time of day, season, and cloud cover. Morning and evening, when the light is less direct and intense, fish will feel more secure—and therefore be more receptive to your fly or lure—at shallower depths than they will at noon. On the other hand, if the sky is overcast, they may feel secure near the surface all day.

*Wind riffle and wave action.* These make fish harder to see from above, so they feel safer close to the surface. Wave action also puts oxygen into the water.

*Where food is.* Comfort and safety are great, but you gotta eat sometime. If fish cannot find enough food at their preferred comfort zone, they will seek food elsewhere. Sometimes this means a quick trip to the surface. After a big meal of hapless insects or small fish, they return to their preferred depth, burping in contentment. It's like Thanksgiving dinner: you have a big meal at the dining table, but when you're done you go back to the easy chair by the fire.

*Fishing Pressure.* When lots of anglers are zipping around the water in their boats, or tossing anchors overboard, or casting lures left and right, fish become concerned and may seek the safety of greater depth.

An important point to remember is that just because there are a lot of fish at one depth, it doesn't mean they are going to be receptive to your lure. Factors such as light intensity or fishing pressure may make them too cautious for successful angling. See the discussion about kokanee in Chapter 7 for an example.

## How to Be Sneaky

People don't understand what it's like to be in the middle of the food chain. Imagine yourself abandoned on city streets at age five with no one to care for you. Every bully, mugger, and pervert regards you as fair game. If you keep your wits and listen to your instincts, you might survive to adulthood. However, you will be one cautious dude. Everybody and everything is going to look like a threat. Even as an adult, you will still have predators to worry about: the IRS, telephone solicitors, car dealers.

From birth, fish are preyed upon by other animals and grow up cautious by instinct and experience. Anglers are just one more predator—clumsy, ignorant, and ill-adapted to pursue fish, but a predator none-the-less.

If you scare a fish badly enough, it swims away. You might see its departure as a dark streaking shadow. More likely, you will be ignorant that anything happened. However, just because a fish did not dash away, doesn't mean it isn't frightened. Fish spend their lives frightened; it's only a matter of degree. If you alert a fish to your presence, it may stay put, but it will become more cautious. The more cautious it becomes, the less likely it will take your lure or bait.

People are visually-oriented and understand that if a fish sees them it might be scared. But fish have other senses, too, and they are much keener than ours. For instance, some fish have a sense of smell almost a million times more sensitive than a person's. They also pick up vibrations in the water through their lateral line, the line that runs along their side. Imagine the side of a fish as being covered with super-sensitive ears and you begin to get the picture. Here are a few of the non-visual things that scare fish or add to their long list of concerns:

*Motor noise and vibration.* Next time you are trolling in an aluminum boat, rest a finger on the hull. Feel that vibration? Fish do, and from a long ways off. Good anglers put out a lot of line when they troll so they can separate motor noise and boat vibration from the lure. Electric motors produce very little vibration. Once they were the exclusive domain of bass anglers, but trout trollers are finding them useful, too.

*Other boat noise.* Sound transmits superbly through water. Fish feel every clank and clunk in your boat, especially if it's aluminum. You can reduce noise through caution and strategically placed indoor-outdoor carpet. If you row, use Teflon oarlocks to keep them from squeaking. Throwing the anchor overboard with a big splash? The fish will probably think the world's largest osprey is after them.

*Bad smells.* You smell bad. So do I. Fish, especially trout, have sensitive noses. There are some obvious fish-scaring no-nos, like motor oil, gasoline, insect repellent, tobacco, and sunscreen. But ordinary human scent is easily detected by fish. Every time you pick up your bait or a lure, you transmit your scent to it. Have you ever taken your wife fishing and been out-fished by her? It might be because she doesn't smell as bad as you (men have more odor than women; that's why mosquitoes are more attracted to men). The answer is not in mouthwash or underarm spray, but in soap. Many outdoor stores sell some kind of angler's soap that removes human scent. Get some and carry it when you fish. Use it often, and wash off your lures as well as your hands.

Besides being quieter and less odorous, there are other ways to be sneaky around fish. Lakes can be very calm. If you cast a fly-line across this calm surface, it lands with a thunk on the water and sends out fish-alerting ripples in all directions. I once cast to a pod of about 60 highly visible trout that were cruising a small bay. There wasn't a whisper of wind, and the water was smooth as polished marble. Until my line hit it. The fish didn't run for the nearest exit. They just moved away from my line. There were fish everywhere—except within 10 feet of my line and fly.

A way to avoid this kind of frustration is to cast over wind-riffled water. The riffles help hide the landing and presence of your line.

Another sneaky thing you can do is fish water that is shaded. Since bright light makes fish more cautious, an area with less light may offer better fishing. When I arrive at a lake, I take a look where the hills and trees are going to shade the water longest at different times of the day—where is the last place the sun will hit the water in the morning, and where will it leave the water first in the evening. In the summer (when the water is warm), those are the places I fish at dawn and dusk.

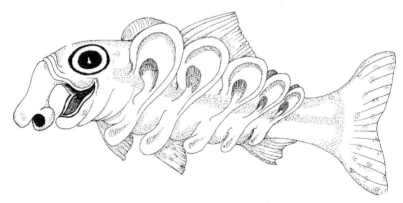

Trout have incredible senses of sight, smell, and feeling. If you imagine them as having a huge nose, gigantic eyes, and big ears all down their sides, you get some idea of how sneaky you must be. (But would you eat a fish that looked like that?)

# Releasing Fish

Several of the Cascade Lakes have naturally-reproducing fish popula-tions, but other than some bull trout and whitefish stocks, there are few indigenous fish in these lakes. Therefore, the need to protect native fish is less here than in many other Oregon waters.

Also, some lakes are over-populated with brook trout and kokanee. The result is stunted fish, recognized by their large heads in proportion to their bodies. In cases like this, taking some fish for your frying pan improves the fishing.

On the other hand, it is not necessary to kill every fish you catch. Before killing a fish, ask yourself: do I really want to eat this guy, or do I just want to show him off? can I keep this fish fresh until I eat it? do I have enough fish to eat already? wouldn't it be great if someone else could enjoy catching this fish, too? Fresh fish can be a delicacy to eat, but there is often more pleasure in catching them than in eating them.

Some of the lakes have mandatory catch-and-release regulations. There are others where I would like to see more fish released voluntar-ily. In particular, I would like to see more big rainbows released at Crane Prairie. This is a unique fishery, capable of supporting many big fish if they are left to grow.

Here are some guidelines for releasing fish:

*Use barbless hooks.* You'll hook (and land) more fish anyway. If your hooks are not barbless, pinch the barb down with a pair of pliers.

*Don't play a fish too long,* especially if the water is warm. Think of the resource, and don't baby that fish. Fly-fishers, take note.

*Use gear appropriate to the size of the fish.* Rods that are too light, or leaders that are too thin, make you play fish to exhaustion. Some anglers think it is "sporting" to use extremely light gear, but sometimes the op-posite is true.

*Wet your hands before handling fish.*

*Back the hook out carefully with your fingers, forceps or needle-nose pliers.*

*If the water is warm, avoid touching the fish at all,* in or out of the water. Leave it in the water and remove the hook with forceps or nee-dle-nosed pliers. In warm water, bacteria and fungus grow quickly. Handling fish—with wet or dry hands, with or without cotton gloves—removes some of the slime coating that protects fish from bacteria and fungus.

*Don't squeeze the fish.*

*Don't hold it by the mouth.*

*Don't put your fingers in its gills or eyes.*

*Don't bring it into the boat and let it flop around.*

*If the fish is hooked any deeper than the lips,* cut your leader, or, if you are using hardware, cut the hook off the lure. Do this immediately; don't fiddle with it. The hook will soon work itself out without harm to the fish. **When a fish is hooked near its gills or deeper, it will probably die if released. Mortality is especially high with small gold-plated treble hooks, such as are often used with traditional Power Bait.** A better catch-and-release strategy for Power Bait users is the "nugget" or "egg" forms that allow you to use a single hook. Even so, if the fish is deeply hooked (in or past the gills), it will probably die withing a few days of being released.

*Don't get the fish tangled up in your net.* There are nets with a soft cotton mesh that are better for catch-and-release fishing, but the best way is no net at all.

*It is best to leave the fish in the water.* If you need to take it out for a photo, keep it out of water for as little time as possible. Recent studies indicate that released fish are three times more likely to survive if they are left in the water than if they are taken out for even one minute.

Holding a fish before releasing it.

*If you need to hold the fish, as for a photo,* grasp it in front of the tail with one hand, and support the head with the other. Your grip will be more sure if you have a cotton glove on the grasping hand, or use a handkerchief. However, note the above warnings about handling fish in warm water.

*To revive a tired fish,* grasp it in front of the tail, as described above, and keep it upright. Pull the fish gently back and forth through the water so that water moves through its gills. Don't let go the first time the fish tries to escape, but wait for the second time. Make sure the gills are working before you let it go.

*If a fish is bleeding when you land it,* or has ingested a hook into its gills or stomach, then you should keep it if the regulations permit.

# 6

# Fishing with Flies

Take a good look at the photos of Bob Jones holding three different brown trout he caught in six hours of fly-fishing on Wickiup Reservoir (page 116). Clearly, the Cascade Lakes offer outstanding opportunities for fly-fishers!

The principles for fly-fishing lakes are the same as for rivers. Anglers need to first, determine where the fish are; next, understand what the fish are likely to feed on and tie on an appropriate fly; and finally, present that fly at the right depth and with the right action.

Chapter 5 covers the first step. The second step—what fish eat and choosing a fly that matches it—is discussed in the next two sections. After that there is a discussion of equipment for lake fishing (including leaders), then fly-fishing presentations are described. The chapter concludes by describing common fly-fishing situations that you will encounter on the Cascade Lakes.

## What Fish Eat in Lakes

Fish are simple creatures who instinctively understand that they will die if they expend more energy chasing their food then they get from eating it. So when a fish looks for food, it looks for "easy pickings," that is, prey that is vulnerable and can't escape.

The human equivalent of a hungry fish is a mugger who only robs cripples as they leave the bank with their life's savings.

This approach to life does not create a moral problem for fish. By concentrating their feeding at those times when their prey is most vulnerable, fish become efficient feeders, and efficient feeding is the path to survival.

Aquatic insects—which are often the main course on a fish's dinner plate—have points of vulnerability that are predictable. Good fly-fishing strategy is choosing a fly and presenting it at the depth and with the action that imitates one of these points of vulnerability.

Aquatic insects are important food for game fish, however they are not the only thing fish eat. Larger fish expand their diets to include other prey, such as smaller fish. There are also fish foods that are not insects, such as crustaceans and leeches. And the wind occasionally blows terrestrial (non-aquatic) food onto the lake.

Common fish prey for the Cascade Lakes are described below. The primary points of vulnerability are discussed for each one.

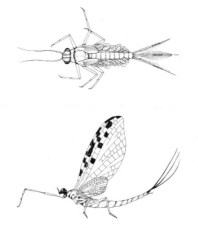

*Callibaetis* **Mayfly**. Mayflies of the genus *Callibaetis* (Cal-ah-beet-us) are the most important mayflies in the Cascade Lakes. Slender and streamlined, *Callibaetis* are good swimmers, the Mark Spitz's of aquatic insects. They flit among underwater vegetation in shallow water, often pausing to crawl along plant stems and munch on some food.

*Callibaetis* **nymph (top) and dun.**

When it is time for them to turn into adults, they swim to the surface and their skin splits open. A winged adult insect crawls out of the nymph case (called a "shuck") and rests briefly on the surface of the water before flying off. This stage of the adult is called a "dun." Duns molt into sexually mature spinners. About a day later, female spinners return to the water and lay their eggs.

The points of maximum vulnerability that you should imitate are: when the nymph is swimming, when it is hatching into an adult, when

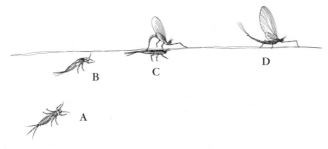

*Callibaetis* hatch. Rising nymph (A), nymph under the surface film (B), hatching (C), and resting dun (D). Each of these four stages represents a different point of vulnerability and is imitated with different fly patterns and presentations.

the dun is resting on the surface, and when the female lays exhausted on the water.

*Callibaetis* begin hatching in late spring and continue through summer, tapering off in fall. At the start of the season, adults are typically about 5/16 inch long (size 12 or 14 dry fly), but as the season wears on they become smaller and lighter in color.

**Midge**. Midge larvae spend most of their time crawling on aquatic plant stems or burrowed into silt on the lake bottom. While fish may eat midge larvae, imitating them is rarely productive. The larva turns into a pupa, which will rise to the surface and quickly turn into an adult. Just after a hatch, midge adults buzz around in great clouds just above the surface of the water.

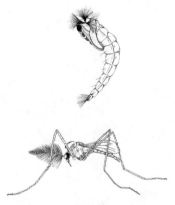

Midge adults are two-winged flies related to houseflies and mosquitoes,

Midge pupa (top) and adult.

but they don't bite. The worst experience you'll have with a midge is to accidentally swallow one (or a bunch). Before you gag, remember there's a lot of protein in insects and that trout do this all the time.

When a midge pupa rises to the surface, it bumps its head on the underside of the lake. The surface tension of the water creates a barrier that most midge pupae, which are tiny, struggle to break through. They

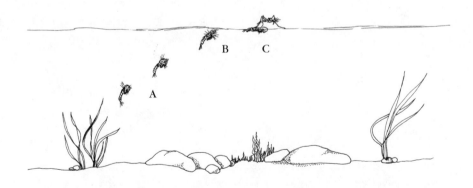

Midge hatch. Rising pupa (A), pupa under surface (B), hatching (C).

push and wiggle for long seconds trying to get to the surface, while hungry fish cruise along and leisurely suck them in. Remember the movie *Jaws?* That's what life is like for a midge pupa.

If a pupa manages to avoid being eaten and gets to the surface, an adult insect crawls out and flies off. Sometimes the newly emerged adults rest briefly on the water, although not for as long as mayflies.

The primary times that a midge is vulnerable to trout in lakes are when the pupa rises to the surface, when the pupa hangs just below the surface, when the adult is hatching on the surface, and when the adult rests on the water.

Midges hatch all year long. Almost every day there is a midge hatch at dusk, often one in the morning, and maybe some midday activity as well. While most midges are tiny (many are too small to imitate), there are some mega-midges out there that are imitated on size 10 or 12 hooks.

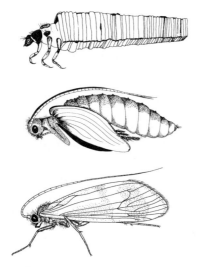

**Caddis.** Still-water caddis are not well understood, and many anglers don't recognize a hatch when it's happening. Fish do, however, and caddis are often the special-of-the-day in the Cascade Lakes' aquatic restaurant.

Two kinds of caddis flies are most commonly found in the Cascade Lakes. The first is about a quarter-inch long with tan wings and a greenish body; it has very long antennae. The second is big, about a half-inch long, and has tan wings and a brown body.

These caddis live among aquatic vegetation. They build tough cases out of plant material and wear them like a sleeping bag. As they go about

Caddis larva in case (top), pupa (middle) and adult.

their daily business, caddis keep their head and shoulders out of the case, but when threatened, they pull into their case like a turtle into its shell. When a caddis nears maturity, it scrunches all the way into its case, seals it off, and turns into a pupa. The mature pupa cuts out of the case, rises to the surface, and a winged adult emerges very quickly.

Unlike most river caddis, these lake species are often found lounging on the water as adults. Some will scoot across the surface like ice skaters doing long glides and occasional figure eights (I've never seen a triple toe loop, though). They make enough ruckus to attract a hungry fish.

Caddis are most vulnerable when the pupa rises, when the adult rests on the surface, and when the adult skates across the surface. They begin hatching in late spring and continue sporadically through summer.

**Damselfly.** Damselfly nymphs swim among aquatic vegetation, often stopping on a weed stem to stalk a bug and eat it. They are vulnerable to fish when they swim, and are large enough to make a good meal.

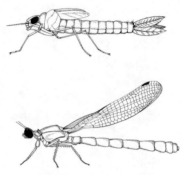

Damselfly nymph (top) and adult.

When they are ready to hatch, damselflies swim in hoards to objects that extend above the surface of the water, such as standing timber, rocks, or plant stems. They crawl up these until they are above the water, then the winged adult emerges. Therefore, unlike the insects discussed above, damselflies are not vulnerable to fish when they emerge. However, fish will gorge themselves on the migrating nymphs, and will feed on the big adults when they return to the water to lay eggs.

Damselfly nymphs live about one year underwater, and are about an inch-and-a-half long when mature. They start hatching in mid-June and continue through mid-July. From the end of July through early August the adults come back to lay eggs in the water, and this can be a good time to cast an appropriate dry fly.

By mid-summer, mature nymphs have hatched. Those that remain are very small and almost translucent. For these reasons, imitating damselfly nymphs works best in the early season.

**Dragonfly.** Big lacy-winged dragonflies, with their marvelous maneuverability, are a common sight on lakes. They buzz along, suddenly stop and hover in one spot, then turn on a dime and buzz somewhere else.

The nymphs of dragonflies, on the other hand, are big and ugly, the sort of thing a young boy throws at his sister to make her scream. Dragonfly nymphs live three years underwater, often reaching two

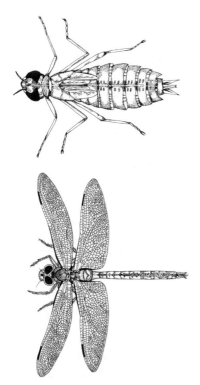
Dragonfly nymph (top) and adult.

inches or more, and feed on other insects.

There are several types of dragonflies. Some burrow in the silt and ambush passing insects, while others are more streamlined and swim among vegetation. There, they pause on a plant stem and stalk other insects. This latter type of dragonfly nymph is what fly-fishers usually imitate.

Like their near-cousins the damselflies, dragonfly nymphs migrate to above-water objects, and the adults emerge in open air. Thus, like damselflies, they are vulnerable when they swim and as they migrate, but not when they hatch. The adults live for several weeks, preying on other insects (especially mosquitoes) and may travel over a mile in search of food. They are such good fliers that they are rarely available to fish.

**Other Fish.** The most common forage fish in the Cascade Lakes are tui chub (roach), whitefish, kokanee, and juvenile trout. Each of these species is a slightly different color and silhouette. They tend to travel in schools and are often found in shallow water when small. Large fish, especially brown trout, will come into the shallow margins of a lake under cover of darkness or low light and feed on these fish.

Except for brook trout and kokanee, all the game fish in the Cascade Lakes will eat other fish. Some, like mackinaw and brown trout, feed heavily on them and can grow to over twenty pounds on that diet.

Because forage fish are often small and frequent shallow areas, they are vulnerable to wave action. The little fish are helpless to resist the push of wind and wave and are gathered onto windward shores, where big fish come in and rip through them like Cossacks through peasants.

Leech.

**Leech.** In the book *The African Queen*, Charlie Allnutt pulls a boat through a leech-infested swamp.

"Just look at the buggers," he says. "Arhh! The beasts!" Trout react differently to leeches; they love them, and a wise fly-angler will always carry a few patterns when fishing the Cascade Lakes.

Leeches are a kind of aquatic worm that swims through the water feeding on vegetation and insects. Most are around two-inches long. All the Cascade Lakes have leeches, some more than others. Few North American species suck blood, however, so there need be no concern about leeches when swimming in these lakes.

Leech patterns can be productive anytime, but real leeches are nocturnal, so the best times to imitate one are dawn and dusk. Common colors are black, brownish-olive, and occasionally red.

**Scud.** Scuds are a crustacean, a kind of olive-colored fresh-water shrimp. They are between a quarter and a half-inch long, and have more legs than seems necessary. They are quite common in some of the Cascade Lakes, and fish feed on them.

Scud.

There are fly patterns that imitate scuds. The Zug Bug is a generic nymph pattern that looks scud-like enough to work. Scuds swim in short erratic spurts near the surface and do not like bright light. Therefore they are best imitated by retrieving a scud pattern in the top three feet of water under low light conditions, such as at dawn or dusk, in shady areas, and on cloudy days.

**Crayfish.** Crayfish are another fresh-water crustacean. They look like little lobsters about two or three inches long and are denizens of lake bottoms (especially in rocky areas). They are jet-propelled, getting their locomotion by taking in water at one end, then squirting it out the other. Crayfish travel backwards (do they ever hit anything?) and settle back to the bottom at the end of each "squirt."

In some of the Cascade Lakes, crayfish are a major part of the fish diet, and most fly-anglers don't recognize their importance. Those that do are understandably reluctant to spend three bucks for a fly they will fish in snag-prone waters. However, a brown or red-brown Woolly Bugger makes a passable imitation and is a lot easier on the pocket book.

**Plankton.** A common food form that cannot be imitated by anglers is plankton. Phytoplankton (microscopic plants) are at the bottom of the food chain. Zooplankton (microscopic animals) feed on phytoplankton, and are in turn fed upon by fish. Kokanee and small trout feed almost exclusively on plankton.

**Terrestrial.** Terrestrials are non-aquatic animals, such as ants, bees, and grasshoppers. Carpenter ants are especially common on the high lakes. By fate or plain clumsiness, a few of these guys get blown onto the water. Many end up in the bellies of cruising fish. I rarely carry a bee pattern, but ants and grasshoppers are always in my fly box.

Take a good look at the surface of the lake on a breezy day. If you notice quite a few terrestrials, you can bet that the fish have noticed them, too, and you might find some success by tying on a matching fly.

**What's in the Water?** There are three secrets to successfully imitating natural food with flies. They are: observation, observation, and observation. Always be on the lookout for what's in the water. Scan the surface and see if anything is hatching. Look for nymph or pupa shucks and check out the size and color. Pick up some submerged tree branches or rocks in shallow water and look at what is clinging to them; many critters you are interested in will be on the underside, away from direct sunlight. Grab a sprig of underwater weeds and see what's clinging to it. See what's flying in the air, or hovering near shoreside bushes.

Floating insects can be darned difficult to extract from the water with your fingers. You need something to strain the water through, such as an aquarium net or a nymph net. The simplest, cheapest, and most compact tool is the end of a nylon stocking. Slip it over your hand like a glove and use it to retrieve bugs from the water.

When you pick a fly to imitate a natural insect, match the size first, then the basic shape, and then the color. When matching size, always measure the insect, then measure your fly. Never guess the size; 90% of the time you will guess one size too big. I usually carry a small plastic ruler marked in millimeters. About every fourth trip I lose it. Then I measure against my fingernails ("Let's see, this guy is about the length of the nail on my little finger, but this other guy is as long as my thumbnail").

Match color by comparing the wet natural to a wet fly; fly patterns get darker in water. Also, many insects are paler on their underside than on top. If you are presenting the fly on or near the surface, the underside color is what you should match because that is what fish will see.

# Fly Patterns for the Cascade Lakes

The fly patterns listed below are well suited to the Cascade Lakes. They represent the major food species and stages that anglers will encounter, and they can be found at most fly shops serving the Cascade Lakes.

Below is a brief description of each fly, grouped by fly type. Tying instructions for each of these flies can be found in Randy Stetzer's excellent book, *Flies: The Best One Thousand*. Of these, there are six "must have" flies that every Cascade Lakes fly-fisher should carry. They are:

Pheasant Tail Nymph or Hares Ear Nymph, size 14 dark brown
Midge Pupa, size 18 black
Woolly Bugger, size 10 olive
Leech, size 8 in both black and brown colors
Damselfly nymph, size 10 olive

## Nymph and Pupa.

*Pheasant Tail.* This is a standard, generic nymph that represents many food forms. The Flashback Pheasant Tail has a strip of flashabou on the back and is an excellent representation of a *Callibaetis* nymph that is ready to emerge. Sizes 12-18 cover the range of most insect forms in lakes.

*Hares Ear.* Like the Pheasant Tail, this is another standard generic nymph. Carry either this pattern or Pheasant Tails in sizes 12-18.

*Zug Bug.* I have a lot of faith in the fish-catching ability of peacock herl, and a fly that is almost entirely made out of that material has got to be good. Zug Bugs are good generic patterns, and make passable scud imitations as well. Carry in sizes 12-16.

*Midge pupa.* Midges are one of the most important food forms in lakes. Carry midge pupa patterns in sizes 16-22. Black, tan, olive, tannish-olive, brown, and dark gray are colors that match common hatches. There are many effective patterns for midge pupae. My favorites are the Jorgensen Suspender Pupa and TDC. A peacock herl that has been stripped of its feathers leaves a tannish-olive ribbon-like stem that can be wound around a hook (size 18 or 20). This makes a good body to imitate a common late season Cascade Lakes midge hatch.

*Deep Sparkle Pupa.* Most caddis in the Cascade Lakes are of two sizes and colors. The pupal form is matched with a Sparkle Pupa pattern. Use it in size 16 with green body and tan shroud, and in size 12 with brown body and tan shroud, and you will cover the major hatches.

*Soft Hackle.* This generic fly looks like a lot of tasty things to fish.

Sizes 12-16 with olive body is best.

*Dougs Damsel.* This is a good, slender pattern that looks like the natural insect. Carry sizes 8-12 in dark olive and light olive. Tie on the color that most closely matches the color of the aquatic vegetation in the lake you are fishing.

*Filoplume Damsel.* One good damselfly pattern deserves another. Carry this in the same sizes and colors as Dougs Damsel.

*Randalls Dragon.* Use this pattern in dark brown and olive colors. Dragons hatch in mid-summer, after which the biggest nymphs are gone. Therefore, pick a size 6 nymph early in the season, but later use a size 10.

**Emergers.** Emergers are insects that are transforming into adults. The first pattern below is fished in the surface film, while the other two are fished like a dry fly.

*Timberline Emerger.* This generic pattern imitates many emerging insects. Carry in sizes 14 and 16.

*CDC Hatching Midge.* An emerging midge hangs briefly at the surface while the adult crawls out of the pupal shuck. It is highly vulnerable, and fish often prefer this stage. Sizes 16-20.

*Hatching Callibaetis. Callibaetis* are the most important mayfly in the Cascade Lakes, and fish can be selective on the emerging stage. Sizes 12-18 cover the range you will see, but sizes 14 and 16 are the most common.

**Dry Flies, Spinners and Terrestrials.** Dry flies are much less important on lakes than on rivers, however fish will take them under the right circumstances. Besides, there is a special thrill that comes with watching a trout suck down a dry fly. Spinner patterns can also be productive; they are fished flush with the surface.

*Adams.* The most venerable and versatile of all generic dry fly patterns. Always have a few Adams in sizes 12-18, either parachute style or upright.

*Elk Hair Caddis.* Caddis of some species will sit on the lake surface for a long time, and cruising fish will sometimes take them. Sizes 14-16 with tan wing and olive body, and size 10 with tan wing and brown body.

*Braided Butt Damsel.* There are a few weeks every year when large numbers of adult damselflies return to the lake to lay eggs. Trout will readily take these big insects when they are available. Bring size 8. Two body colors—blue and black, and green and brown—are commonly found in these lakes.

*Griffiths Gnat.* This imitates an adult midge or a cluster of two mating adults. It sometimes produces well when midge pupa patterns will not. Sizes 18 and 20.

*CDC Callibaetis Spinner.* Sometimes fish focus on these adults as they return to lay eggs. Sizes 14-18.

*Daves Hopper.* Grasshoppers are occasionally blown onto the water and are big enough to make a real meal for fish. Size 8.

*CDC Ant.* Like grasshoppers, wind-blown ants are sometimes available to fish. Size 14 black.

## Streamers and Other Patterns.

*Marabou Leech.* Leeches are "must-have" patterns. Good leech patterns have most of their weight in the front half so the fly will travel in an undulating path when it is retrieved. Size 8 or so (not too important), but carry both black and brown. Olive can also be a productive color.

*Woolly Bugger.* This popular generic pattern imitates a lot of critters: damsel nymphs, dragon nymphs, leeches, baitfish, crayfish, or just something that might be good to eat. You can't have too many Woolly Buggers. Carry sizes 4-10 in olive, brown, and black.

*Carey Special.* For decades, this has been a favorite pattern of northwest lake fishers. Does it imitate dragonfly nymphs? Baitfish? Damselflies? Who knows? It sure does work, though. I think those feathers just flutter around in the water, making the fly look like something alive and juicy. Size 8.

*Scud.* Most of the Cascade Lakes contain scuds, and it is a good idea to keep a few in your fly box. Size 12 olive.

*Woolhead Sculpin.* A good pattern if you are pursuing fish-eating species like brown trout. Size 2 is best, although it's about as easy to cast as a full-grown Persian cat.

*Zonker.* This fly represents a lot of baitfish, from chub through kokanee. Size 6 covers most bases.

*Muddler.* The versatile muddler minnow is another excellent baitfish imitator, but it has bouancy (unlike the Zonker) and is usually fished in shallower water. Sizes 6-10.

*Matuka.* A big streamer that has caught a lot of brown trout.

*Crayfish.* Sometimes a crayfish pattern fished near the bottom can be effective.

# Tackle

**Rods and Reels.** A five- or six-weight rod is sufficient for most fishing in the Cascade Lakes. If you are pursuing early season mackinaw or trophy brown trout, you might think about a seven- or eight-weight rod. On the other hand, if you are going to a lake with small fish, you might get by with a four-weight. Rod choice is largely a matter of balancing the ability to make long casts into the wind and play heavy fish, against the ability to protect thin tippets and have fun with small fish. That, and a lot of personal preference.

I favor a pair of nine-foot six-weight graphite rods. This seems to be a versatile rig for most lakes I fish. There are times when I wish I had a five-weight, but other times I've linked up with trout that made me glad for the stouter rod. I own a nice little three-weight, but I rarely use it on lakes because it dies if there's any wind.

Reels are something I never think about unless they break. To me, the less noticeable a reel is, the better I like it. I look for a durable model that has good drag control, lets the line come off easily when a fish runs, stands up to some weather and abuse (I'm always dropping reels onto rocks), and has interchangeable spools at a reasonable price. The latter is so I can carry several different lines. Beyond that, I don't want to have to think about my reel except to lubricate it occasionally (and usually not frequently enough).

There is one time when I like my reel to come out of obscurity and be noticed: that's when I hook a nice fish that peels line off the spool. Then I want a reel that sounds like a duck that just got stepped on. I have friends with reels that cost more than my first car (a '57 Rambler; not worth much, actually). These fancy reels make no noise at all, so I'm not interested in them. I go to a lot of work to hook a nice fish. When that guy makes his run, I want an audible reward even if I'm alone.

**Lines.** When I fish a river, I rarely use anything but a floating line. But on a lake, I carry two reel frames and five spools, each with a different line.

One of the lines is a floater. I prefer a double-taper line because it lets me flick out a little roll cast to start a new cast. This picks the line up from the water with less fish-scaring fuss. Other anglers prefer a weight-forward line because it casts a little farther.

My other four lines are sinkers, each of which drops at a different rate. Sinking lines are of two primary types: sink-tips, where only the last 10 or 20 feet sink and the rest floats; and full-sinking, where the

Keep your eye on the fly!

whole line sinks. Some people favor sink-tips, but I prefer full-sinking lines because they are better at keeping the fly at the correct depth. Also, there is more of a straight line between me and the fly, which results in fewer missed strikes. Each line sinks at a different rate, so I change lines depending on how deep I want my fly. Sinking lines come in weight-forward tapers.

Because I have all these lines, I take two rods with me. This increases my chances of having the right line for the immediate situation. Also, if I don't have to re-string a rod, I am more likely to switch to a different strategy rather than stick with one that's unproductive. On the other hand, I've got more gear in my way.

If you only carry one sinking line, make it an intermediate line. They sink very slowly, which let's you fish just below the surface (where an awful lot of action happens), or if you are patient enough, a few feet deeper. With this line and a floating line, you can address many fly-fishing situations.

Some anglers use a shooting-head system. That way they can

change lines without changing reels or re-stringing a rod. That's definitely an advantage when you're in a float tube, especially if you have a long rod and short arms. The disadvantages of this approach are that the line does not stay as well at the preferred depth, and the joint between the running line and the shooting-head creates a hinge between you and the fish. That hinge must straighten out before you can tighten up on a fish and set the hook.

**Leaders.** Leaders separate your highly visible fly line from the fly and transfer casting energy from the line to the fly. Tippets, the very last part of the leader before the fly, are measured by "X" size. The "X" size is determined by subtracting the diameter, in thousandths of an inch, from 11. Thus 3X is .008 inches thick (11 minus 8 is 3). A useful rule of thumb is to choose a tippet size that is equal to the fly size (on a standard dry fly hook) divided by three. So a size 12 dry fly would match a 4X tippet.

However, this is just a starting point. Often, the conditions dictate a different choice. If the water is exceptionally clear, or the fish very spooky, you might need a thinner tippet than would be ideal. For instance, you might tie a size 10 damsel nymph to a 5X tippet. On the other hand, if you are casting size 22 midge pupae to five-pound rainbows, you'll want a stronger tippet than 6X or 7X.

Another variable is leader length. For most situations, a nine foot leader is a good starting point if you are using a floating or intermediate sinking line. But if the water is clear or the fish are easily frightened, a longer leader is better. I never venture onto Crane Prairie or Hosmer Lake with a leader shorter than 12 feet, and I'll often go to 15 feet.

For other sinking lines, four-foot leaders are the starting point because the shorter leader keeps the fly down with the line. Again, you might lengthen the leader a bit if the water is quite clear.

Always maintain at least two feet of knot-free tippet. I know that when I change flies often, it isn't long before my tippet is only a foot long and I'm not getting any strikes. When I clip off the old tippet and add a new three foot section, fishing usually picks up again.

Keep your leader straight. If it has more kinks than your cousin's sex life, it won't straighten out enough for you to feel a fish on the other end. Stretch the leader between your hands. If it still won't straighten, hold a piece of inner tube or India rubber (available in most fly shops) between your fingers. Pinch the leader in the middle, and pull it through.

# Presenting The Fly

There are many ways to present a fly to fish. In all cases, the fly should be at the correct depth (see Chapter 5) and have an action that resembles a living creature. The presentations discussed below are the most common and effective ones to use in the Cascade Lakes.

**Chuck-and-Sit (dry fly).** This presentation should be used when you are imitating adult caddis, hatching midges or *Callibaetis,* ovipositing (egg-laying) damselflies, the spinners of *Callibaetis,* and occasionally during a midge hatch.

Dry fly presentations in lakes are tricky. The fish have a lot of time to look at your fly, and the act of casting disturbs the water, especially if it is a calm day. Therefore your fly needs to be well tied and your presentation needs to be subtle.

Before you start casting a dry fly, make sure the fish are really feeding on the surface. Often what looks like surface rises are actually fish feeding a few inches underwater. Even when fish are taking insects off the surface, they'll usually be just as enthusiastic about a well-presented subsurface fly—and they will be more forgiving of your mistakes.

Use a floating line, and dress both the line and the fly with floatant. Cast your fly to a likely spot and let it sit. If nothing has happened for a minute or so, give the fly a little twitch by pulling on the line just enough to make a few ripples around the fly. If there is still no action, cast to a new spot.

If you see a cruising fish, cast ahead of it so your fly and line have time to settle before the fish arrives. If you are not sure which direction the fish is cruising, cast quickly to the center of its last rise. During a hatch, it is often better to wait until you see a rise, then immediately cast to it. On the other hand, if you have trouble making a cast that lands gently on the water, you will be better off not casting close to rising fish. In this case, place your cast and wait for fish to come to you. That way things can quiet down without a fish watching.

One of the problems with dry fly fishing in lakes is the disturbance the fly and line make when they are picked up for the next cast. If you are using a double taper floating fly line, you can minimize this disturbance by doing a small roll cast first (this doesn't work well with a weight-forward line). This lifts the fly and line from the water so you can make your normal backcast and presentation. Keep your line well dressed with floatant and your pick-up will be smoother.

If you seem to be spooking fish with your presentation, try casting to water that has been wind-riffled. The disturbed water will help conceal your cast. Sometimes rising trout are difficult to spot in wind-riffled water, and it takes an act of supreme faith to turn your back on obviously feeding trout in calm water, and cast instead to water where fish are not apparent. The results should bolster your faith.

**Subsurface Emerger.** This is the same as the chuck-and-sit, but you don't dress the fly with floatant. That way it hangs just below the surface and looks like a midge pupa, Callibaetis nymph, or other emerging insect.

There are two problems you will encounter with this presentation. One is getting the fly underwater. Small unweighted flies like midge pupae don't have the mass to break through the surface film and often end up sitting on top of the water looking as natural as a fish strolling through the parking lot. Often, you can get the fly under if you give the line a quick pull. Unfortunately, this can make a fish-scaring fuss on the surface. Sometimes you can make a fly sink by spitting on it before casting. Another approach is to tie a fly with a minuscule amount of lead on it, but that can spoil the profile of the fly. There are commercial leader-sink compounds; some of this stuff gooped onto the last six inches of leader can do the trick.

The other problem is having your fly sink too much. Putting floatant on the leader (except the last four to six inches) can often take care of this.

**Rising Nymph.** This presentation imitates a midge or caddis pupa rising from the bottom to the surface. It can also be used during a *Callibaetis* hatch, although I think there are better strategies then.

Use a sink-tip line or floating line with a long leader and weighted fly. Cast to a likely spot and wait for the fly to sink. Then slowly retrieve line so the fly will be pulled to the surface. This kind of vertical retrieve seems especially effective with brook trout.

**Count-Down-and-Strip.** This is a subsurface presentation and imitates the behavior of a lot of fish food. It is what you will use most when fishing the Cascade Lakes. A sink-tip or full-sinking line is best. It is possible to use a floating line with some flies, especially if they are weighted, but if the water is calm the line will make fish-alerting ripples.

Cast your fly and count until the fly reaches the proper depth, then strip in line in a manner consistent with the type of food you are repre-

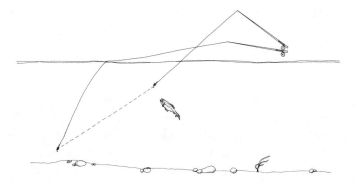

In the rising nymph presentation, lift the rod or strip in line so the fly rises smoothly and steadily toward the surface.

senting (shown below). What should you count to? Count to whatever depth you catch fish at. If you start hooking bottom or weeds, come up a little. In shallow lakes, the fish will usually be found either near the surface or at the weed tops.

Retrieval speed and action are very important. Below are some starting points for imitating the natural motion of different fish prey. However, these are only starting points, and it is good to vary the speed and action of the retrieve. Early season when the water is still cold, a slow, barely moving retrieve is needed. Later in the season, an unnaturally fast retrieve may be the only approach that hooks fish.

Here are starting points for stripping speed and action:

*Damselfly nymph.* Strip in about one foot of line in two seconds. Pause two seconds, then do it again.

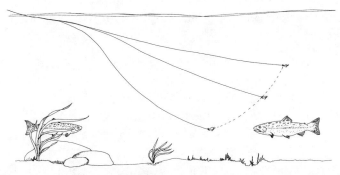

One of the most useful presentations in lakes is the count-down-and-strip. Use a sinking line and let the line and fly sink until they reach the desired depth. Then strip in line to give motion to the fly.

*Dragonfly nymph.* Retrieve 2-6 inches of line in one second. Pause briefly and repeat.

*Leech.* Pull in about 24 inches of line in two seconds, pause briefly and repeat.

*Scud.* Retrieve line in short, erratic strips.

*Crayfish.* Retrieve about three feet of line in a steady, moderately fast pull. Then let the fly settle for about five seconds and repeat.

Float tubes are the ideal platform for this retrieve because you can impart action by kicking with your fins. Also, you can retrieve line while slowly kicking, thus giving your fly action as well as covering the water.

**Slow Retrieve.** A slow retrieve of a nymph or pupa just under the surface can be very effective, particularly during midge and *Callibaetis* hatches. Sometimes it imitates the behavior of emerging insects, while at other times it may just focus a trout's attention on your fly. A slow retrieve of a damselfly nymph, presenting the fly just at the weed tops in a shallow lake, can be deadly.

Use a floating or intermediate line, and an unweighted or lightly weighted fly. Make sure the fly is under the surface film. Retrieve very slowly—about an inch or two of line each second, or less—or slowly troll with your float tube. Most strikes will be subtle and will feel like a slight hesitation or stickiness.

The right time to use this retrieve is when fish are actively feeding, and frankly, most people don't have the patience for it. I know I sometimes don't. When you see rises, the natural tendency is to speed everything up. Telling yourself to go slow when you are surrounded by big feeding fish is like putting a 16 year-old boy in a room with a naked lady, then telling him to close his eyes and think about his religious upbringing. It can be done, but there are many forces of mind and body that tug against it.

**Lift and Settle.** This presentation can be effective during midge hatches, and sometimes in the period prior to a *Callibaetis* hatch. Cast a sinking fly on a floating line with a long leader (about 15 feet), or use a sink tip line. Slowly retrieve enough line to raise the fly a few feet. If there is no take, stop retrieving and let the fly sink; then repeat the action.

Some fly anglers use a strike indicator, such as a small corkie or a piece of foam tape. Put the indicator on the leader near the fly line. If this reminds you of fishing with a worm and bobber, you're doing it right.

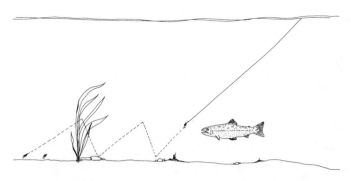

The lift-and-settle presentation can be effective during a midge hatch, especially when it is midday and the fish are not comfortable near the surface.

## Special Fly-Fishing Situations

**Midge Hatch**. The wind has stopped, and the sun is slipping behind a mountain, leaving the lake in a golden glow of fading light. You can hear the forest coming alive for the night. The smooth surface of the lake is broken by a rise ring. Half a minute later, another one appears. Soon, they're all over the lake. Sometimes you see the dorsal fin and tail of a trout, often not. You take a long look at the mountain peaks as they turn red in the sunset, but your eye is caught by a movement on the lake: a few hundred yards away, an angler has raised her rod and a trout jumps.

Some of my fondest fly-fishing moments come from sitting mid-lake in a float tube at day's end, watching this quiet, peaceful hatch unfold. The hatch is subtle and understated. It's such a perfect end for the day, that I usually don't care if I catch anything. That's a good thing, because matching this hatch can be frustrating.

There are so many species of midges (over 1,000 in North America), and each species is so abundant, that you can plan on a midge hatch nearly every day throughout the fishing season. The most common hatches occur in the evening and gather intensity right up to dark.

Hatches can also occur in the morning and sometimes in the middle of the day. While midges are important to fly-fishers year round, they are especially so in September and October when other hatches have tapered off.

Midge hatches are recognizable by the following features:

*Fish are rising* and making dimples on the surface or porpoising (head and tail rises).

*Many of the rises are mid-lake,* in water too deep for most aquatic insects.

*There are few insects resting on the water,* but there are clouds of small insects flying an inch or so above the surface.

*If you look closely* you can see small, two-winged insects crawling out of their pupal shucks on the surface.

Midges are most vulnerable to fish as they rise, when they hang just under the surface, and as they hatch. The first case is imitated using a midge pupa pattern and the rising nymph or lift-and-settle presentations. The second is imitated with the same fly, but use the emerger or slow retrieve presentation. In the last situation—a hatching midge—use a fly of that name and a chuck-and-sit presentation.

The biggest challenge of a midge hatch is to match the size and color of the emerging insects. Snare yourself an insect, as discussed earlier in the chapter. Carefully compare it with your flies, and pick one that's the exact size and approximate color as the real insect. Given a choice, match size before color, since fish are more tolerant of color differences than size. Get several insect samples, because more than one midge species may be hatching at the same time.

Some anglers will present two or three midge pupae at a time, as shown below. This does two things: it increases the odds, since your fake fly is only one among thousands and thousands of real ones, and it lets you experiment with different sizes and colors to see which is preferred. However, this rig is a pain to cast without tangling, so don't try it unless your casting skills are good.

Three midge pupae on one leader. The flies hang on the leader between blood knots spaced about a foot apart.

Most people think all midges are small, but some of the early season species are quite big and are matched with a size 10 or 12 hook. There are occasional late season hatches of similar sized midges.

Doing well in a midge hatch can be difficult. Matching the natural insect is often tricky, and because the hatches usually occur when the water is flat, your presentation has to be good. If you find yourself getting frustrated, take a break and enjoy the peace and the scenery.

*Callibaetis* **Hatch.** Nearly all the Cascade Lakes have a population of *Callibaetis*, but shallow lakes with lots of aquatic vegetation, such as Hosmer and Crane Prairie, are noted for their large hatches.

You can tell when a *Callibaetis* hatch is in progress by the large number of newly-hatched adults (duns) resting on the surface. When their wings are dry, they will fly off.

As stated earlier, the times when *Callibaetis* are most vulnerable to fish are when the nymphs swim near the surface, when they hatch, when the dun rests on the surface, and sometimes as spinners. To imitate the first case, use a nymph such as a Flashback Pheasant Tail. Good presentations for this stage are lift-and-settle, emerger, and slow retrieve, the later being my favorite. In the second case, use a Hatching *Callibaetis* pattern with a dry fly presentation. For the third case, use a dry fly presentation and a Parachute Adams or similar fly (a tannish-olive body is best). To imitate spinners use a fly with outspread wings and a gray-brown body; fish it flush in the surface film.

When fishing a dry fly in still water, I prefer (and think the fish prefer) as little hackle as I can get away with. Most store-bought flies have too much hackle for lakes, so I use the scissors on my Swiss army knife to trim the fly to the point where it barely floats. The best dry fly for this hatch is a No Hackle pattern, but you can only hook a couple of fish before the fly is too torn up to use.

From one day to the next, *Callibaetis* hatch at about the same time of day, usually between 10 AM and 1 PM, but sometimes later. If you fish a lake one day and see a *Callibaetis* hatch, note the time of day. Odds are there will be another hatch the next day at about the same time. The hatch lasts a couple of hours, but an overcast day can spread it out over a greater time.

Several hours before the hatch starts, the nymphs become quite active and fish feed on them subsurface. This creates an extended opportunity for fly-anglers, who can start fishing the nymphs well before the actual hatch cranks up.

One of my preferred *Callibaetis* strategies is to work a Flashback Pheasant Tail nymph on an intermediate sinking line so it travels just below the surface. I give the fly a slow retrieve near weeds and shallow margins beginning a couple of hours before the duns will emerge. Even during a hatch, this tactic can be more productive than fishing dry flies, but I often switch to dries regardless because . . well, just because.

**Damselflies**. Take a close look at the standing snags in Crane Prairie in August. You will see that they are covered with what look like dried out bugs. These are the nymph shucks from which adult damselflies emerged. The number of shucks gives some idea of how many damselflies live in this lake. When you consider their numbers and their size, you can imagine how much food is moving through the water. No wonder the fish get big here!

Any lake with submerged weedbeds will have damselflies, so they are a good pattern to have in your box. During the pre-emergent migrations, fish gorge themselves on the nymphs. Fly-anglers can imitate the nymphs' behavior by casting a fly and retrieving it toward standing timber or similar above-water objects. But don't confine your fishing to migration times. Fishing the nymphs is a good strategy from early season through July.

By August, nymph activity has tapered off. This is because damselflies are single-brooded, meaning this year's adults will not have mature progeny until the following year. Thus, after mid-summer, damsel nymphs are not readily available and fish are looking for other food.

Earlier in this chapter I described how to retrieve damselfly nymphs. This is only a starting point, and it doesn't hurt to experiment with different retrieves—some fast, some slow. Fish in different lakes seem to respond differently to retrieval speed. Crane Prairie, which is especially rich in damselflies, has trout that seem most receptive to a very slow retrieve just over the weed tops.

Jim Dexter, who owns a fly shop on US 97 in La Pine, loves to fish damselfly nymphs in the Cascade Lakes. A few Julys ago, Jim was in his float tube fishing a favorite piece of Crane Prairie damsel water. He was picking up a four or five-pound rainbow every 15 or 20 minutes (Jim is world-class, so don't be disappointed if your success rate is lower). A nearby angler was fishless, and noticing that Jim's rod was often bent double, he carefully came over to see what the secret was.

Jim is one of the most innovative fly tiers in the Northwest, and favors a very sparse streamlined pattern for these nymphs. He showed the man his fly. "Too thin!" cried the other angler. Jim showed him his retrieve, which is so slow it makes glaciers look like greyhounds. "Too slow!" cried the other angler, and went back to catching nothing. Jim shrugged his shoulders and went back to catching several four and five-pound rainbows every hour. Sometimes you can't be too thin or too slow.

**Caddis**. Few fly-anglers recognize the importance of still-water caddis, but these insects can provide some excellent fishing. As discussed earlier, the Cascade Lakes hold two primary kinds, one about a quarter-inch long and the other about a half inch.

When caddis emerge, the pupa fills a membrane with gas and rises quickly to the surface. The case immediately splits open, and an adult comes out and flies off. Because the adult requires almost no wing-drying time, it doesn't linger on the surface exposing itself to fish like mayflies do.

Caddis hatches look like midge hatches, except the caddis don't hover over the surface as midges do.

Some caddis hatches occur at dusk and are simultaneous with midge hatches. This can create confusion. You might try every midge strategy in the book and have few takers because the fish are focused on rising caddis pupae. Furthermore, much of the activity may be obscured because the fish are taking pupae underwater.

Fishing a pupa pattern with a "rising nymph" or "lift-and-settle" retrieve can be effective during the hatch. Use a steady, moderately fast retrieve to pull the fly towards the surface.

Sometimes a dry fly, such as an Elk Hair Caddis is also productive. Most Elk Hair Caddis are tied for use on rivers and have enough hackle to float a small rock. But you are on a lake, and, as with *Callibaetis* patterns, the less hackle the better. Give the fly a haircut by trimming the hackle off the bottom. That way it will sit down flush in the water and look more natural.

There is another effective way to fish a dry caddis, though few anglers actually do it. These caddis sometimes run across the water. You can imitate this behavior by stripping in some line, pulling your fly across the surface. The resulting fuss attracts fish, who think "easy meal" and smash the fly.

When skating a fly like this, you need it to sit up above the water so it will move easily. Therefore the fly needs lots of hackle, and you can't use one of those flush-sitting jobs that you use for a "chuck-and-sit" presentation.

**Leeches**. The midge hatch had waxed and waned, ending about 15 minutes after sunset. It was getting dark, so I got my headlamp out of the back of my float tube and turned it on. I clipped off the midge pupa and tied on a black marabou leech. I cast the fly and gave it a strip-pause-strip-pause retrieve as I kicked my way back toward Crane Prairie's Rock Creek Campground.

About half way back, the rod bent double and line ran from the reel. It took over ten minutes to bring the big rainbow in, and it was no picnic to play a fish that size in low light amid a forest of standing timber. Before releasing the lunker trout I measured him against the scale on my float tube. The scale goes to 22 inches, but this fish extended well past the last hash mark.

While fishing in low light has many frustrations, the rewards can be high. Leeches are a staple for lake fish, but the aquatic worms are nocturnal and anglers should be prepared to fish them most heavily around dawn and dusk.

In Oregon, you can fish from one hour before sunrise to one hour after sunset. It can get pretty dark on the Cascade Lakes even 30 minutes after the sun goes behind a mountain, regardless of when official sunset happens, so be prepared with a flashlight and some leech patterns to use after the midge hatch has faded.

Most leeches are brown, black, or olive, although you occasionally see a red one. Usually it doesn't matter if you fish a brown one or a black one at dawn or dusk, but if you cast a leech during the daylight hours, the difference between the two colors can be profound. I once fished a black leech for several hours with little success. I switched to a brown one and couldn't keep fish away from it.

# 7

# Fishing With Bait and Lures

This chapter describes the pursuit of fish with bait and lures. The first section details a basic approach to still-fishing with bait. The next discusses fishing with lures in general. The last two sections focus on using lures to catch kokanee and mackinaw.

As stated in the introduction to this book, most of my lake fishing is done with flies. I occasionally use spinners for trout, spoons for trout and kokanee, and plugs for trout and mackinaw. However, I do not consider myself an expert on these techniques. Therefore, to make sure that the last three sections are accurate and usable I have leaned heavily on the advice of experts, especially Jed Davis. Jed is familiar to many anglers through his column in *Salmon, Trout, Steelheader* magazine and his landmark book, *Spinner Fishing for Steelhead, Salmon, and Trout*. Jed is a superb and rigorous thinker about fishing for salmonids, and deserves full credit for most of the ideas presented here on fishing with lures for trout, kokanee, and mackinaw. I recommend Jed's writings to anyone interested in pursuing cold-water game fish in any type of water.

## Still-Fishing With Bait

In the Cascade Lakes, most still-fishing for trout takes place in water that is 10 to 30 feet deep. Much shallower than that and you are too obvious to the fish. Much deeper and you are fishing where there are few fish.

Some people have the notion that fish are found in "holes," and so they fish in the deepest part of the lake they can find. This is a poor strategy because few trout feed below 30 feet. Sometimes they go deeper in search of cooler, more oxygenated water, but in general, bait-fishing should concentrate in the 10-30 foot range.

Once you have located a good place (see Chapter 5), your next still-fishing challenge is being *still*. If your boat swings in the wind, it is difficult to tell when a fish has taken your bait. Therefore it's best to carry two anchors. When you come to a likely spot, steer the boat into the

---

wind and put out a bow anchor. Then let out more anchor line than you need and let your boat drift backwards. Once the boat has settled, put out a stern anchor, then pull up on the bow line and tie off both the bow and stern anchor lines. This way the boat is suspended between the two anchors and will stay in one place (mostly).

Waves are another problem encountered by still-fishers. Too much wind and wave action pulls on the line, and it becomes hard to detect a bite or keep the bait in one place. If this happens to you, your best strategy is to find more sheltered water or wait for the wind to die down. Most of the Cascade Lakes are calm in the mornings, making it a good time for still-fishing, but some of the larger lakes can become rough from mid-afternoon through evening.

**Using Power Bait.** When I was a boy, I often fished for carp in Seattle's Lake Washington. A favored bait was a doughball made from flour, water, and various smelly substances thought to attract fish. A gob of this odorous goo was molded onto a hook and cast into the water, where the smell attracted fish.

Well, the doughball concept has gone high-tech in the form of Power Bait, the brand name for a chemical concoction from Berkeley Tackle. Its properties are that it floats while slowly dissolving and emitting a smell that attracts fish and stimulates a feeding response. Given enough time in the water, Power Bait will dissolve into nothing. One advantage is that it does not spoil; however it will dry out if the jar is left uncovered. Power Bait comes in a variety of colors, the most popular of which are chartreuse and fluorescent red.

To fish with Power Bait, take a small amount from the jar and mold it onto a gold treble hook so it just covers all the hook. Don't use too much. The hook should be small—size 16 or 18—so your hunk of bait will be small enough for a fish to easily get it into its mouth. A treble hook is necessary to keep the bait from falling off.

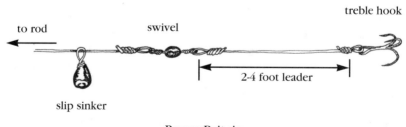

Power Bait rig.

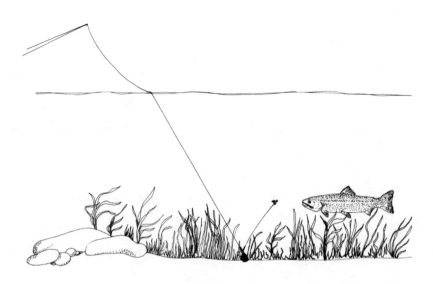

With leader of the right length, floating bait like Power Bait or worms and marsh-mallows rests at the level of the weed tops—a prime cruising zone for fish.

The advantages of this setup are that the bait will float up from the bottom and, if the leader is the right length, rest just above the weed tops. As a fish pulls on the bait, the line slides through the sinker so the fish doesn't feel the sinker's weight.

As you can see, leader length is very important. Too short and your bait is in the weeds; too long and it rests beyond the weed tops, above the prime cruising zone for hungry fish.

Cast your rig away from the boat (or bank, if you are fishing from shore) and let it sink. After the rig hits the water, close the bail on your spinning reel (or keep your bait casting reel from free-spooling). Otherwise the leader and line tend to twist together as they sink.

Once your bait is in place, put some slack in your line and hold the rod still; this is the hard part for kids, who seem compelled to wave the rod around like an orchestra conductor. Watch the line and wait patiently for jerks in the line or for the line to move away. This is not a fishing technique for Type A personalities! If there are no takes after 15 minutes or so, reel in slowly (sometimes fish follow the bait before taking it) and cast to a different place. If you have covered the water near your boat and have not gotten any action, move to a new spot.

If you have tried several locations and are not catching fish, use a different color of Power Bait. Sometimes that makes a difference. You might also try changing the length of the leader, since it is difficult to judge the height of the weeds, and you want to be at that prime place along the weed tops.

Users of Power Bait should recognize that this fishing technique is incompatible with catch-and-release fishing. Power Bait is potent stuff, and fish tend to ingest it. They are usually hooked too deeply to remove a hook, and a gold-plated treble hook that is lodged far down the gullet takes a while to dissolve, even if you cut the leader. If you hook a fish with Power Bait, it's yours.

Berkeley Tackle recently introduced two new varieties of Power Bait, called Power Nuggets and Power Eggs. It is the same stuff as traditional Power Bait, but comes in discrete chunks like salmon eggs. The advantage of these products is that you can use single hook, which is not as lethal to the fish (see Chapter 5 about releasing fish hooked with bait).

**Worms and Marshmallows.** Before there was Power Bait, there were worms and marshmallows. Tackle stores sold (and still sell) jars of miniature marshmallows in unnatural colors. The marshmallow is put on a size 6 or 8 worm hook, then a nightcrawler is threaded on. Other than the hook, the rig and presentation are the same as for Power Bait. The colored marshmallow serves to visually attract fish and to float the real bait, the nightcrawler.

**Bobbers.** The venerable bobber still has a place in lake fishing. The advantage of using a bobber is that your bait is a fixed distance from the surface, rather than a fixed distance from the bottom (as with the techniques described above).

Common baits to use are worms, salmon eggs, and dragonfly nymphs. Dragonfly nymphs are often called "hellgrammites" by bait-fishers who don't know any better. Hellgrammites are actually the nymphs of alderflies, and other than being big and having six legs, they don't look much like dragonfly nymphs. If you want to watch a fly-fisher turn red in the face and treat you like an ignorant boob, call a dragonfly nymph a "hellgrammite" in his presence.

Bobbers should be as small as possible. Otherwise they interfere with the strike. Also, fish often take bait very subtly, and a large bobber masks what is happening.

When fishing this way, don't put any sinkers on your leader. Just let the bait settle naturally into position. Obviously you need bait that sinks, so floating Power Bait or worm/marshmallow rigs don't work.

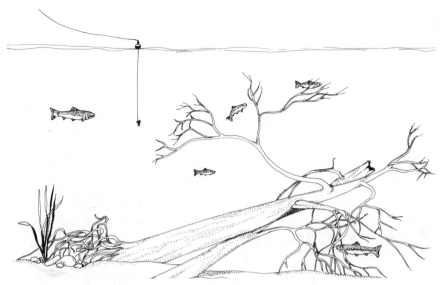

A bobber lets you fish from the top down. This is an advantage when the bottom is littered with snags or when fishing near the bottom would put you too deep.

**Fishing from the Bottom Up or from the Top Down?** When you fish a lake with bait, you have to decide if it is better to fish from the bottom up, such as you would with Power Bait, or from the top down, as you would with a bobber. This decision is even more fundamental than your choice of bait.

Some of the Cascade Lakes are very deep, and fishing off the bottom can put you below the fish. However, there may still be fish cruising around in the top 15 feet of water, even though the bottom is 30 feet below them. Another reason for fishing from the top down is that the bottom may be littered with downed timber and other gear-catchers. Fishing from the top down puts you above this tangle.

On the other hand, if the fish are in 20 feet of water and are cruising the weed tops, the bottom-up approach is a better tactic.

## Fishing with Spinners, Spoons, and Plugs

When I was very young, I talked my grandmother into taking me fishing off a pier near her home in Vancouver, B.C. I had heard that spoons could be used to catch fish, and so convinced her to tie a kitchen spoon to the end of some string. She was dubious, but I was a young boy in need of amusement, so she humored me. We went to the pier, where I dangled my rig in the salt water and watched schools of fish swim past it like it was invisible.

After a while, I began to have doubts about the efficacy of my tackle. I clearly remember thinking, "I don't see how a fish is going to stay on, even if it tries to eat my spoon." This is my earliest conscious memory of fishing.

Since then, I've found out a few things about spoons, as well as spinners and plugs. For one thing, they attract more fish when they have some motion, either from trolling or from casting and retrieving. And then there's this thing called a "hook" that makes the fish stay on.

**Spinners.** Spinners have long been popular and effective lures in the Cascade Lakes. In fact, if someone told me that ancient Indians canoed around these lakes pulling lures with twirling black blades made from obsidian, I'd probably believe it.

Spinners are easy to cast and retrieve, so they are well suited to beginning anglers. On the other hand, an expert spinner angler is as skilled and knowledgeable as an expert fly-fisher.

Some anglers believe that spinners imitate minnows, and that's why trout and other game fish take them. This is incorrect. Spinners are pure attractors, imitating nothing. They emit light flashes and vibrations which excite a fish and may induce a strike response.

Fish can detect the flash and vibration from a wide radius, and the larger the spinner, the larger the radius within which it will be detected by fish. Therefore, anglers should use as large a spinner as they can get away with. However, different environmental conditions or feeding habits may cause the fish to want a smaller or less flashy lure. In his book *Spinner Fishing for Steelhead, Salmon, and Trout*, Jed Davis calls this the "The Threshold of Attraction." Basically, you want your lure to be exciting and attractive to fish, but not so exciting that they are spooked or put off.

The question naturally arises, How much excitement can a trout stand? The answer is not simple and depends on a number of factors, most of which are environmental. Because fish are cold-blooded, their metabolism—which is a major factor in how excitable they will be—is driven *primarily by water temperature*. For trout in the Cascade Lakes, temperatures below 50 degrees slow their metabolism to the point where it takes a lot to excite them. Above 68 degrees, oxygen concerns start to play a role in their behavior, and their interest in food and lures begins to taper off. Between 50 and 68 degrees (the most common situation in the Cascade Lakes) they are comfortable and more easily attracted.

The effect of temperature on trout behavior varies depending on the strain of fish, as well as the species. The Cascade Lakes are stocked with trout that are more tolerant of temperature extremes than their native coastal cousins, so references to the impact of specific temperatures do not apply to waters on the west side of the Cascades.

The intensity of light that reaches fish is another strong influence on their behavior. Some of the factors involved include the time of day (less light in morning and evening, more at noon), season (lower sun angle in spring and fall), the amount of particles and debris in the water (if the water is murky, more light is absorbed and less reaches the fish), cloud cover, and shade.

At times, increased lighting can be a great detriment to success. Suppose you are fishing a lake on a warm and windless day in August when the water temperature is 65 degrees. The sun is high and the lake is as smooth and clear as glass. Where are the trout? Hiding under rocks, hunkered down in deep water, or sulking in some other low-light place that makes them feel secure. The combination of warmth (increased metabolism) and bright light (decreased security) means the threshold of attraction is low. Under conditions such as these, fish will not leave their lairs except for a lure that is small, dark, and toned-down.

On the other hand, you could fish the same spot on a sunny day just after ice-out. Because the water is cold, the fishes' metabolism is lower, so they are not as put off by the bright light. Their threshold of attraction

---

### Effect of Water Temperature on Threshold of Attraction

| Below 50° | 50° to 68° | Above 68° |
|---|---|---|
| Low metabolism, high threshold of attraction | Variable threshold of attraction | High metabolism, low oxygen, low threshold of attraction |
| Large flashy spinners can be used. | Spinner choice should be based on lighting, water surface, water clarity | Use small, dark spinner |

is high, and a large, flashy spinner could be used.

Besides light intensity and temperature, some other factors to consider include:

*Fishing pressure.* It makes fish feel less secure.

*Depth.* Under summer conditions, fish are less secure in shallow water if the surface is calm and unbroken.

*Wind riffle and wave action.* These break up the light and offer a type of overhead cover.

*Maturity of fish.* Smaller fish require more food for their size and are more likely to abandon caution in the pursuit of food.

*Time of year.* For example, brook trout are very aggressive in spring, just after ice-out.

*Buying a Spinner.* When I fish the Cascade Lakes, I carry three sizes of spinners: 0, 1, and 2. I carry blade and body combinations in each size as follows: silver blade, silver body; brass blade, brass body; silver blade, black body; brass blade, black body; and black blade, black body. This gives me a range of sizes and brightness so I can match different fishing conditions.

Sometimes I put a piece of Kelly green reflective tape on the blade of the silver/silver or brass/brass spinners. This has the effect of coloring the flash emitted by the spinner. Store-bought spinners sometimes come with colors on the blade, but often the colors are aimed more at luring anglers than fish.

I confess that I'm not happy with store-bought spinners; they cost more than I want to pay, and I can't always find the finishes I want. The cost makes me reluctant to cast them around weed beds, rock piles, and submerged logs for fear I'll loose one. But those are precisely the places that fish hang out. That's why I make my own spinners from materials I buy from Pen Tac, a mail order company in Seattle. It's a lot cheaper, and the product is better. However, if you choose to buy your spinners, look for the sizes and finishes discussed above.

When buying a commercial spinner, make sure the blade of the spinner extends past the body, and that the spinner blade turns e̶ when you retrieve it.

|  | Blades | | |
|---|---|---|---|
| **Bodies** | Silver | Brass | Black |
| Silver | X | | |
| Brass | | X | |
| Black | X | X | X |

The author's preferred body and blade color combinations for lake fishing.

Hooks are another feature to pay close attention to when you buy a spinner. Look for a wide-bend "French style" hook with a short shank, such as are found on the Mepps and Blue Fox spinners. This style costs a little more, but it hooks and holds fish better. If you are serious about fishing with spinners, give some thought to buying these hooks in bulk quantities (they're VMC 9649BZ trebles) and putting them on commercial spinners. Compared to how much money you spend on gas, lodging, food, etc., a few extra pennies for a decent hook is peanuts.

*Which Spinner to Fish With.* Most anglers select a spinner based on gut feel, so their lure choice is more driven by indigestion than by science. A methodical approach to spinner selection is as follows.

Remember, the goal is to use the largest, brightest spinner you can so you can attract fish from the widest possible radius. But environmental factors influence both the metabolism of the fish and the amount of light that reaches them, and if your lure has too much flash, it will exceed the "threshold of attraction" and limit your catch.

The four major factors to consider when you select a spinner are:

Water temperature
Lighting
Water surface
Water clarity

If the water temperature is cold (below 50 degrees), a trout's metabolism slows and a bigger, flashier spinner can be used. A #2 or even #3 with a silver finish is appropriate. Silver has the greatest visibility and flash, so it has the best chance of exciting a trout into striking. If the temperature is between 50 and 68 degrees, a trout's metabolism is higher and the fish may be put off by a too bright spinner. In this case, select a smaller lure, such as a #1.

Lighting is the next factor to consider. The more light that reaches the fish, the smaller and less flashy the spinner should be. But remember, water temperature comes first! Cold water negates bright conditions. For example, if the water is 40 degrees, sunny conditions are not much of a factor.

Water surface affects the intensity of light that reaches the fish. If the surface is choppy or riffled, less light will reach the fish, and a bigger spinner can be used. Under calm, glassy conditions and bright sun, use a smaller spinner.

Water clarity is another factor that affects the intensity of light reaching the fish. If the water is clear, more light passes through to the fish and a smaller spinner is called for. If the water is murky, a bigger one can be used.

So before you select a spinner, measure the water temperature, scan the sky, look at the water surface, and peer into the depths. Consider all four factors together, then pick your spinner.

---

### How Environmental Factors Affect the Threshold of Attraction for Trout in the Cascade Lakes
#### (Water temperature between 50 and 68 degrees)

| Condition | Raises Threshold (Use larger, flashier spinner) | Lowers Threshold (Use smaller, toned-down spinner) |
| --- | --- | --- |
| Water temp | Low | High |
| Lighting | Overcast, dawn, dusk | Bright |
| Water surface | Chop or riffle | Calm |
| Water clarity | Murky | Clear |

---

*Spinner Tactics.* Once you have chosen a spinner, tie it to a leader about 18 inches long with a swivel between the leader and the main line. If your store-bought spinner already has a swivel, you can tie it directly to the line. Do not use a snap swivel to attach the spinner to the leader because that makes it harder to feel the spinner's action.

Spinners can be cast or trolled. I usually cast mine, either from shore or from an anchored boat. Sometimes I just let the boat drift in the wind while I cast. That way I can cover a lot of water without fiddling with the anchor or dealing with the odor and noise of a motor.

Cast to water that you suspect holds fish (as described in Chapter 5), and let the spinner sink. Count the seconds while it sinks. That way you can consistently reach the same depth, or methodically change to a new depth if your initial guess doesn't produce fish.

When the spinner is at the chosen depth, retrieve it. Retrieval speed should be varied until you find one that catches fish, then stay with that speed. The best speed is often the one that gives the slowest flash (slowest spin of the blade) but still maintains the correct depth.

---

Often, a change in lure speed and depth induces a strike, and an effective tactic is to stop reeling and let the lure sink a couple of feet before resuming your retrieve. This is one way of dealing with fish that follow your lure but don't take it.

**Spoons.** Like spinners, spoons are attractor lures that reflect light and emit vibrations. The difference is that spoons produce flash and vibration by wobbling back and forth rather than spinning.

Some spoons are meant only for trolling and are too small and light to be cast. Some brand names are Needlefish, Superduper, and Triple Teaser.

Bigger spoons can be trolled alone, or cast. Because they are usually heavier than spinners, large spoons can be trolled more deeply without extra weight. When cast, they sink faster than many spinners, stay down better when retrieved, and can be cast a long distance. But when they hit the water, they make a bigger, fish-scarring ka-splooosh. Also, big spoons reflect a lot of light since they have so much surface area, so it's easy to have too much flash and exceed "the threshold of attraction." Therefore, toned-down colors are often better.

The proper color choices for spoons are similar to those for spinners. Spoons often come in colors, and some are painted to look like fish, such as perch. Don't think of these spoons as fish imitations, however. Think of the color in the same way you would think of a spinner that has had reflective tape added to it, as described earlier. It is a way of coloring the flash emitted by the lure.

The tactics for casting and retrieving spoons are basically the same as for spinners: if you cast them, count down the seconds before you start to retrieve so you can hit a specific depth with consistency; then vary the speed of your retrieve until you find what works best. With spoons, you should have a distinct "thump-thump-thump-thump" in your rod tip. This means you are getting the slow flash you want.

**Plugs.** What does a plug look like to a fish? For many plugs, the advertising hype is that it "looks like a wounded baitfish." Have you ever seen a wounded baitfish? Did it swim quickly through the water wagging its tail at 300 rpm? Probably not. A wounded baitfish is more likely to swim in a spiral pattern. I've yet to see a plug that did that. Some plugs look like healthy baitfish, but I've never seen a plug that I thought looked like a wounded baitfish.

Most plugs used in the Cascade Lakes are "crankbaits." They have a lip in front that makes them wiggle from side-to-side when retrieved or trolled.

Flatfish, Kwikfish, Hot Shots, etc. are crankbaits that are pure attractors. They stimulate fish primarily through vibration and movement, though reflected light is important, too. Since these are attractor lures (rather than imitative), color choices should be based on the available light: silver in sunny, well-lit water; gold if there is high overcast; green, blue, or purple on a dark day or in shadows.

Other plugs, such as Rapalas, Rebel Minnows, and Jensen Minnows are minnow imitations. They look like baitfish swimming through the water about as much as most trout flies look like the insects they imitate. In the Cascade Lakes, these plugs are most often used for brown trout, and the local wisdom is to choose a plug that looks like the baitfish that are available to the fish you are pursuing. Thus, anglers in Paulina Lake usually use black and silver or blue and silver lures that looks like the kokanee that are common in the lake. But in neighboring East Lake, a lure with gold or yellow on it is preferred because the dominant baitfish is believed to be chub.

If you buy a Rapala to represent chub, get one of the jointed models rather than the traditional straight kind. Traditional Rapalas are best suited to a fast troll of three to four miles per hour, but the jointed lures troll best at a slow speed, which is a better imitation of a chub's swimming motion. Also, chub are fat fish (they are "chubby;" these things make sense when you think about them), and the jointed style presents a more realistic silhouette.

All plugs need to be checked to make sure they run straight (track true). Tie the plug to your line and put it over the side of the boat while you are at trolling speed. The plug should be stable and not wander off to either side when trolled at the highest speed at which you will use it. If it is not tracking straight, bend the connector loop with pliers until it runs true.

Plugs are usually trolled, but many casting plugs are commercially available. These allow you to cast into coves and other areas that are hard to reach by trolling.

**Trolling Spinners, Spoons, and Plugs.** Trolling in Northwest lakes has traditionally meant pulling a rig with several bright spinning blades followed by a #8 hook with a worm on it. The theory was that you attracted fish by presenting them with the gaudiest, flashiest, most visible rig you could devise. Then the fish would investigate all the bright lights and discover the worm. This was a good try, and there is a certain logic to it. It works often enough that I suspect some anglers will go to their grave before they give up their five-bladed lake trolls.

However, many anglers are discovering that simpler rigs are often more effective—and provide better sport. As was pointed out in the section on spinners, too much flash and dash can be counter-productive, frightening rather than attracting the fish.

Jed Davis did a thorough investigation of this issue on Odell Lake. On one downrigger he used a simple rig with just a small spinner and eight red beads ahead of the hook. The hook had a single piece of corn over the point. On the other downrigger he ran the same spinner with a traditional, commonly-used lake troll in front of it. Over a six week period, the plain rig out-produced the traditional one by more than four to one. Furthermore, the plain rig caught bigger fish. What happened?

Jed explains it this way. "The turbulence of those trolls is so great that it moves the big fish to the sides. When the troll has gone past, the big ones are too spooked to come back. The little ones are less shy and more aggressive for food, so they assume the original position first. Therefore, they are the first ones to encounter your troll and most likely the first ones to bite. Thus, you get smaller fish."

Jed adds, "There is still another factor to consider in the case against lake trolls. Traditionally, we give fish much less credit than they deserve for being able to see our offerings. In a clear lake such as Odell, I am quite convinced that kokanee are aware of my offering even if they are holding 15-20 feet deeper than I am running my rig. Thus the necessity for long parades of tinsel trains is overkill and works against an angler's

For man or beast, trolling can be a relaxing way to fish.

efforts to attract quality fish."

Besides terminal tackle, the two other big issues in trolling are depth and speed. Some rigs are trolled near the surface, but others need to reach fish at a specific depth, as discussed in Chapter 5. Traditional approaches using lead weight on the line are inaccurate. The trolling depth will vary depending on how much lead you put on and how fast you troll. This is why I favor downriggers. With a downrigger, you know just what depth your rig is at, and when you get a strike, you can play the fish without encumbering weights. For under $100 you can buy a workable downrigger that can be clamped to the side of a small boat. If you're serious about lake trolling, take a long look at downriggers. I was devoted to mine five minutes after I started using it.

Trolling speed is the other issue. Some species of fish, such as mackinaw, seem to prefer a slow troll. One morning on Cultus Lake, I noticed an angler who was hooking a lot more mackinaw than I was. I followed him in my boat to see how fast he was trolling. I turned my throttle down as far as it went and crept along at a frustratingly slow pace. I was still overtaking him. This guy was moving at the speed of a crippled snail. When I got close, I saw he was using an electric motor to achieve the slow speed.

On the other hand, under summer conditions large rainbows and brown trout often prefer a fast troll, about three-and-a-half to four miles per hour, with thin-bodied plugs such as the traditional Rapala. But if the water is cold, as at the extremes of the season, these fish prefer a slower troll.

Once you have chosen a nominal depth and speed, recognize that changing one or both of these will sometimes induce a fish to strike. A good way to change depth and speed is to troll in wide "S" curves.

Trolling in "S" curves varies the speed and depth of your lure. These changes can induce a fish to strike.

When on the inside of the curve, a lure will travel more slowly and sink; while on the outside it will go faster and rise. In this way you cover a variety of depths and speeds, while creating the kind of changes that entice fish.

An exception to the "S" curve tactic is when your lure is near the weed tops. It will sink into the weeds if it goes too slow.

# Fishing for Kokanee

Kokanee are land-locked sockeye salmon. While they are native to some northwest lakes, they are an introduced species in the Cascade Lakes. They don't get large (18 inches is a trophy fish), but they are excellent eating. In some lakes where they spawn naturally, kokanee have over-reproduced, resulting in stunted fish. In these lakes, you can improve the fishing by taking a limit of kokanee to put in the frying pan or smoker.

**Finding Kokanee.** Kokanee feed only on plankton (microscopic plants and animals) that they strain from the water. Kokanee tend to travel in schools at depths where they find their food supply. Therefore, mature kokanee will concentrate in certain areas of a lake, and within those areas they will bunch up into several groups of fish. However, they follow their food supply and can change position quickly.

Serious kokanee fishers use an electronic fish finder to locate the concentrations of fish and determine the depths they are at. Anglers who do not have sophisticated electronics in their boat should check at the local resort. Every kokanee fishery in the Cascade Lakes has a resort nearby. Ask where the fish are and at what depth (you need answers to both questions). The resorts get this information from successful anglers and consider it their business to pass it on to others. Use this as a starting point, but keep in mind that it isn't necessarily the gospel. You can also look around the lake for the largest concentration of boats in the early morning. Often (but not always) that's where the kokanee are being caught.

In some lakes, almost all mature kokanee are found near the same depth. But sometimes they occur in tiers. For reasons I don't fully understand, this is particularly true at Odell Lake, where you might see active kokanee on the surface, then the fish finder shows several large schools at 25 feet, more at 45 feet, and a few more down around 80 feet.

In situations like this, it is important to realize that the shallower fish are likely to reject your lure if the prevailing light is bright and the lake surface is calm. If conditions change, such as more wind and wave action or cloud cover, the shallower fish will feel more secure and may suddenly become receptive to your offering. The reverse is also true; calmer water and/or brighter light may turn shallow fish from eager biters to sullen lock-jaws.

**How to Get to the Right Depth.** You have three choices for getting down to the fish. They are, in order of increasing desirability (and investment):

> Lead weight on the line
> Lead core line
> Downriggers

To use lead weights, rig up as shown below. Use 2 oz. of lead if the fish are under 30 feet deep, and 4 oz. if they are deeper. The advantage of this rig is that it is the cheapest. The biggest disadvantage is that it is difficult to know just how deep your lure is, and that's a disadvantage that can kill your fishing. You let out line and start fishing at some unknown level, and every time you change your trolling speed your rig will change depth.

Another disadvantage is that you have to play the lead weight as well as the fish. If you have a heavy rig, it becomes difficult to tell the difference between the kokanee and the weight. You can always tell the kokanee fishers with four ounces of lead, a five blade lake troll, and a heavy-duty rod to handle it all. They're the ones that have conversations like, "Gee, I don't know, Earl. Do you think there's a fish on that line? Maybe we should reel in and see if we caught anything."

Lead core line is available at most full-service tackle dealers. Typically the color of the line changes every 10 feet. If you troll slowly, lead core line can get a lure down without extra weight, but you still don't know exactly how deep you are fishing. Furthermore, the depth will vary with trolling speed.

Downriggers are the best solution. I can't say enough positive things about fishing with downriggers. They take the guess-work out of trying to hit a specific depth, and they let you use light-weight rods that are better matched to the size and fight of kokanee. Most makers of downriggers offer (relatively) inexpensive portable models that can be

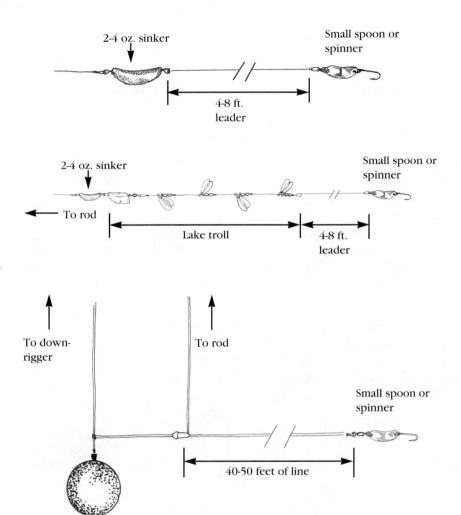

2-4 oz. sinker

Small spoon or spinner

4-8 ft. leader

2-4 oz. sinker

Small spoon or spinner

To rod

Lake troll

4-8 ft. leader

To down-rigger

To rod

Small spoon or spinner

40-50 feet of line

**Three kokanee rigs: lead and lure (top), lake troll (middle), and downrigger.**

mounted or clamped to the gunwales of small boats.

With a downrigger you can control the depth precisely, and when a fish strikes you can free your line from the weight. When I fish for kokanee, I use an ultra-light spinning rod and a small spoon. I connect this to the downrigger, and when a kokanee hits I have something that resembles sport.

**Choosing and Presenting a Lure.** Kokanee are plankton eaters, but you can't put a gob of plankton on the hook for bait. Therefore, catching kokanee is a matter of inducing a strike reaction to something that is outside of their eating habits. Most angler-caught kokanee are mature fish ready to spawn in the coming fall. Apparently they take the lure out of territorial aggression. If they didn't, you'd never catch a kokanee on rod-and-reel.

Popular rigs consist of a dodger or lake troll, followed by a small lure (usually some kind of spoon) for terminal tackle. The biggest functional difference between a dodger and a lake troll is that a dodger imparts action to the lure, as well as emitting flashes of light. If you are using a lure that has action of its own, such as a spoon, don't use a dodger for an attractor.

As I said in the trolling section, I'm not a big fan of either dodgers or lake trolls. You can catch more and bigger kokanee without them, and they are just one more thing between you and the fish. Fishing without a dodger or lake troll is heretical to some kokanee anglers, but it works better.

Put a single kernel of white corn on your lure so it covers the hook point. All the resorts at kokanee lakes sell little packages of white corn. It won't take much for a day or two of fishing.

Traditionally, kokanee fishing was done with four ounces of lead and a big lake troll. This required a heavy-duty rod. As a result of this approach, a lot of fish were lost on the strike, and kokanee developed a reputation for having a soft mouth. In reality, the problem was due more to the stiff rod than to the kokanee's mouth. If you use a light-weight rod with a flexible tip, the rod will absorb the shock of the strike. But if your rod is stiff or you think you are losing fish on the strike, you can put a rubber snubber in the leader; these are available at most tackle stores.

**Jigging for Kokanee.** Jigging requires simple equipment and is an effective tactic for catching kokanee as well as mackinaw. A jig is a heavy lure, often shaped like a fish, although this is not necessary.

Good jig colors are white, black and white, green and white, and pink and white. Black and white is probably best for deep jigging. One or two ounce jigs are sufficient for kokanee.

To fish a jig, position your boat where you think kokanee are schooled up and lower the jig till it hits the bottom when your rod tip is at the surface. Then raise your rod a few feet and drop it suddenly back to the surface. The jig should flutter down sideways. This part is critical, and is achieved by lowering the rod quickly. When you do it right, loose line briefly piles up on the surface until the jig drops and tightens it. Kokanee usually hit the jig while it is sinking.

After the jig has dropped and tightened the line, pause a couple of seconds, then repeat the process. That's it—nothing very tricky except finding the fish and keeping the jig fluttering in front of them.

It is possible to jig for suspended kokanee—those that are not hovering near the bottom. However, jigging works best when the water is calm, and calm water combined with bright sun means that suspended kokanee are not as receptive as those on the bottom in deep water. Therefore, jigging off the bottom usually catches more and bigger fish.

Sometimes you see people jigging by suddenly raising the rod, causing the jig to move upwards very fast. This is not a good jigging technique. Sometimes the people who do this are snaggers. Snaggers want to drop the jig into a school, then rip the jig through the middle of them, hoping to snag a fish before it has a chance to get out of the way. Snagging is an illegal fishing method used by anglers who lack the skill and moral fiber to catch fish by legitimate means.

## Fishing For Mackinaw

Mackinaw are also known as lake trout. They are not a true trout, but are a member of the char family. They grow slowly, but live long and can reach huge sizes; the state record is a 40 pound fish from Odell Lake. Because mackinaw can be big fish, you need to take along a salmon net when you pursue them.

Mackinaw are related to bull trout, which are a protected species in Oregon. The skin of a bull trout has an olive tint, whereas mackinaw are a grey color. Also, mackinaw have a more deeply forked tail than bull trout (see picture in Chapter 5). All bull trout must be released unharmed.

Small mackinaw (under 12 pounds) make the best eating. Because they have so much body fat, mackinaw must be properly prepared to taste good. Strip out the fat that lines their bellies and middle before cooking them. Barbecuing is a good way to cook mackinaw because it renders the fat.

**Where To Find Mackinaw.** Mackinaw are fish eaters. Their primary foods in the Cascade Lakes are kokanee, whitefish, and chub, although they will take small fish of other species if they are available.

Mackinaw can tolerate very deep, cold water, and can be found as far down as 300 feet. In whatever lakes they are found, mackinaw have a definite preference for water that is 48-52 degrees. A good rule of thumb is that mackinaw hold on the bottom where the water is about 51 degrees. They prefer areas with structure, such as boulder fields, rocky outcrops, volcanic cones, ledges, and drop-offs. They wait in these places and ambush passing baitfish.

Once you think you know where mackinaw are, the next challenge is getting a lure down to them. This can be quite a trick when they are in water over a hundred feet deep. The methods are the same as for kokanee: lead on the line, lead core line, or, preferably, a downrigger.

When fishing for bottom-lying mackinaw, a fish finder is essential because you need to set the downrigger so your lure will travel within three to six feet of the bottom. As you troll, you will need to continually adjust the downrigger as the depth changes. Also, remember that a diving plug such as a Kwikfish or Flatfish will travel deeper than the downrigger ball. To reduce the likelihood of lures hanging up on the bottom, some mackinaw anglers remove the front hooks. Another approach is to run the plug off a stacker release five feet above the downrigger ball.

Mackinaw are not always found in deep water. For a week or two after ice-out, they can be found preying on small fish in shallow areas near islands, points, or other shoreside structure. At these times, they can be caught on cast lures, or even with a fly rod.

**Choosing and Presenting a Lure**. A large lure is essential. Common choices are U-20 or M2 Flatfish or a large Kwikfish. Silver and blue lures seem to work well, although some successful anglers swear by silver and black plugs.

As stated in the section on trolling, lake trolls and dodgers are usually counter-productive. Mackinaw can find your lure just fine without them. But if you just feel naked without some big flashy thing, use a silver/brass model. If you are trolling a fly or other lure that does not have action of its own, use a dodger to impart motion. Otherwise, use a lake troll. But you will probably do better with neither.

When presenting a lure to mackinaw, troll slowly, with just enough speed to give good action to the lure. Macks like it slow. Real slow. You wouldn't believe how slow they can like it. If Mackinaw were people, they'd be corpulent couch potatoes, the kind that would watch the same TV channel all day if the batteries died in the remote control.

Other than speed, the most important thing to remember about

A sunrise troll for mackinaw on Cultus Lake.

trolling for mackinaw is to stay near the kind of structure and temperature zone they favor.

Traditionally, mackinaw anglers used stiff rods and big reels. The advent of downriggers, however, allows the use of lighter gear, such as a good steelhead rod and a level wind reel filled with 12-15 pound monofilament. This makes mackinaw fishing more enjoyable and sporting.

Also Available from

## FLYING PENCIL PUBLICATIONS

FISHING IN OREGON'S DESCHUTES RIVER by Scott Richmond
An award-winning guide to fishing—and to caring for—the lower Deschutes.
Detailed and practical. "By the time you add up the text, photos, maps, line drawings, and hatch charts, you have a single thorough source to help you get the most
out of this great river." —Santiam Flycasters
173 pp. 6 x 9, paperback                              $12.95 ISBN: 0-916473-08-2

THE POCKET GILLIE by Scott Richmond
A practical vest-pocket handbook guaranteed to expand your understanding of
where to look for trout, how to choose a fly with confidence, and how to adapt your
tactics to fit the trout's feeding expectations. "A perfectly splendid book." —Nick
Lyons
216 pp. 4 3/4 x 6 1/2, paperback                      $14.95 ISBN: 0-9633067-0-7

FISHING IN OREGON by Madelynne Diness Sheehan and Dan Casali
The 8th edition of this award-winning guide to more than 1200 Oregon lakes,
rivers, and bays. Richly illustrated with dozens of maps and photographs. Available
after September, 1994. "The one essential planning aid...best single source of information." —Field and Stream
240 pp. 8 1/2 x 11, paperback                         $18.95 ISBN: 0-916473-10-4

FISHING THE OREGON COUNTRY by Frank Ames
An introduction to the state's abundant fisheries by an Oregon fishing master. Frank
Ames explains how to fish the state the year around. "A timeless collection of practical Oregon fishing know-how." —Maddy Sheehan, author of Fishing In Oregon
230 pp., 5 1/2 x 8 1/2, paperback            $10.95 ISBN: 0-916473-02-3

STEELHEADING FOR THE SIMPLE-MINDED by Bob Ellsberg
An enjoyable, lightly written how-to. Offers tips on tackle and techniques that will
let you slip confidently into the streamside line-up your first day out. "Imparts a
good deal of fishing wisdom without losing its sense of humor." —Sports Afield
86 pp., 5 1/2 x 8 1/2, paperback             $ 6.95 ISBN: 0-916473-04-X

FISHING WITH SMALL FRY: How to Hook Your Kids On Fishing by Bob Ellsberg
A refresher course in kid-fishing techniques, good natured tips on streamside par-
enting, and plenty of encouragement. "Wonderfully illustrated and the perfect
guide for introducing your children or grandchildren to the world of fishing. —Pat
McManus
119 pp. 5 1/2 x 8 1/2, paperback.                     $9.95 ISBN: 0-916473-07-4

Use your credit card to order by phone
**1-800-858-9055**
*When ordering direct from the publisher, add $2 for shipping a single book. Add
$1 for each additional book.*

## FLYING PENCIL PUBLICATIONS
33126 SW Callahan Road, Scappoose, OR 97056